C000096654

Jellies, Jams, Preserves and Conserves

by Marion Harris Neil

Copyright © 2013 Read Books Ltd.
This book is copyright and may not be
reproduced or copied in any way without
the express permission of the publisher in writing

British Library Cataloguing-in-Publication Data
A catalogue record for this book is available from the
British Library

Preserving and Canning Food: Jams, Jellies and Pickles

Food preservation has permeated every culture, at nearly every moment in history. To survive in an often hostile and confusing world, ancient man was forced to harness nature. In cold climates he froze foods on the ice, and in tropical areas, he dried them in the sun. Today, methods of preserving food commonly involve preventing the growth of bacteria, fungi (such as yeasts), and other micro-organisms, as well as retarding the oxidation of fats that cause rancidity. Many processes designed to conserve food will involve a number of different food preservation methods. Preserving fruit by turning it into jam, for example, involves boiling (to reduce the fruit's moisture content and to kill bacteria, yeasts, etc.), sugaring (to prevent their re-growth) and sealing within an airtight jar (to prevent recontamination). Preservation with the use of either honey or sugar was well known to the earliest cultures, and in ancient Greece, fruits kept in honey were common fare. Quince, mixed with honey, semi-dried and then packed tightly into jars was a particular speciality. This method was taken, and improved upon by the Romans, who *cooked* the quince and honey - producing a solidified texture which kept for much longer. These techniques have remained popular into the modern age, and especially during the high-tide of imperialism, when trading between Europe, India and the Orient was at its peak. This fervour for trade had two fold consequences; the need to preserve a variety of foods - hence we see more 'pickling', and the arrival of sugar cane in Europe. Preserving fruits, i.e. making jams and jellies became especially popular in Northern European countries, as without enough natural sunlight to dry food, this was a fail safe method to increase longevity. Jellies were actually most commonly used for savoury items; some foods, such as eels, naturally form a protein gel when cooked - and this dish became especially popular in the East End of London, where they were (and are) eaten with mashed potatoes. Pickling; the technique of preserving foods in vinegar (or other anti-microbial substances such as brine, alcohol or vegetable oil) also has a long history, again gaining precedence with the Romans, who made a concentrated fish pickle sauce called 'garum'. 'Ketchup' was originally an oriental fish brine which travelled the spice route to Europe (some time during the sixteenth century), and eventually to America, where sugar was finally added to it. The increase in trade with the sub-continent also meant that spices became a common-place item in European kitchens, and they were widely used in pickles to create new and exciting recipes. Soon chutneys, relishes, piccalillis, mustards, and ketchups were routine condiments. Amusingly, Worcester sauce was discovered from a forgotten barrel of special relish in the basement of the Lea and Perrins Chemist shop! As is evident, the story of food preservation, and specifically the modern usages of jams, jellies and pickles encompasses far more than just culinary history. Ancient civilisations, nineteenth century colonialism and accidental discoveries all played a part in creating this staple of our modern diet.

JELLIES, JAMS, PRESERVES
AND CONSERVES

BAGS FOR STRAINING JELLY

JELLIES, JAMS AND PRESERVES

" Ripened fruit gleaming red like precious rubies "

Jellies are cooked fruit juices and sugar, boiled together nearly always in equal proportions, and the process of jelly-making does not differ materially in any case.

The secret of successful jelly-making lies in the careful observations of a few simple directions which must be followed exactly or the jelly will be cloudy, ropey or thin.

Two substances are necessary for jelly-making. One of these is pectin, which in fruit corresponds to gelatin in animal substances. This will not work without acid, hence we find it difficult to make jelly of such fruits as the peach without the addition of lemon or tartaric acid or combining with other acid fruits.

There is less pectin in dead ripe fruits than in partly ripe fruits.

Overripe fruit and cheap grade sugar will never make good jelly.

Crabapples, quinces and grapes have plenty of pectin, so much so that extraction may be used. For instance, juice may be taken from the grape, water added to the residue, and jelly made from this juice.

If too much sugar is used in jelly-making the jelly will run and be soft; if not enough, the jelly will be tough. There is no difference in cane and beet sugars for making jellies.

The shorter the time of boiling, the more distinct will be the particular fruit flavor.

Too much water in cooking the fruit injures the quality of the jelly.

A perfect jelly should be of good taste, color and texture.

The most satisfactory jelly test is to drop the hot jelly from a cold spoon. When it just "jells" the hot syrup should be transferred at once to hot glasses previously well sterilized with boiling water. The glasses should be filled completely, then set in a cool place for the contents to harden.

Cover with hot paraffin and clean covers, and keep in a cool, dry place. Or the paraffin may be shaved and put unmelted into the hot glasses and the hot jelly poured over it. This will melt and rise to the top, and form a smooth coat. When the jelly is cool it is ready to set away. This saves time and also the cleaning of a paraffin pan.

The kinds of bags used for straining the juice are important. Three kinds are needed, made respectively of mosquito netting, cheesecloth, and flannel or felt.

Jellies, Jams and Preserves

The mosquito net must be doubled, cut in a square of about fifteen inches, and stitched into a three-cornered bag with a double seam and turned-in edges. A strong tape should be fastened to each side to form a loop across the top.

The cheesecloth may be cut into squares and hemmed or made into triangular shaped bags, and the flannel should be triangular in shape and hemmed with double seams.

The work of straining juice through a jelly bag can be greatly simplified in the following way: Put the fresh fruit into the bag and place in a preserving pan with the proper quantity of water. Cook until the fruit is soft, then hang up the bag to drip. Or boil the fruit in the pan in the usual way, and when done turn into a colander, then strain only the juice through the bag.

When jelly seems a little too thin after it is in the glasses, instead of boiling it over again put the glasses in a pan and set them in the oven for a few hours or set them out in the sun. The jelly will thus generally attain the proper thickness, and have a better flavor and color than when cooked longer.

For all soft fruits try this new way of making the jelly: Late in the afternoon take the fruit, place it in a large earthenware bowl, and mash it well. Add one-half as much water as juice extracted. Let stand over night. In the morning the juice will have collected on the top. Pour it into a preserving pan, leaving the sediment which may be made into jam in the bowl. Boil the juice for a short time, then add the heated sugar and continue to boil until it jellies. Divide into scalded jelly glasses and seal with paraffin.

There are several ways of preventing jam or fruit butters from sticking or popping out of the pan. One is to put two or three sterilized marbles in with the fruit and by their constant movement they will keep the fruit from adhering to the bottom of the kettle.

Another way is to rub the inside of the kettle with fresh butter or olive oil before putting the fruit in, rubbing off the superfluous grease. Still another is to set the pan of fruit in a deep dish of boiling water, then it can cook for any length of time without scorching.

Mixed jellies are now quite popular. Strawberry and rhubarb, gooseberry and strawberry, raspberry and currant are all pleasing combinations.

No housewife should use preserving powders when preserving or canning fruits or vegetables as they are unnecessary and dangerous and should be absolutely avoided.

Many people like the delicate flavor imparted to jellies and preserves by the addition of a few cracked kernels of the peach, plum and cherry stones; but the cook should remember that this flavoring must be used very moderately in order to leave no unhealthful

Jellies, Jams and Preserves

effect. These kernels contain the same principle that gives the flavor to bitter almonds, an alkaloid that forms the base of that most deadly poison, prussic acid. When enough of these kernels are added to preserves to make the almond-like flavor pronounced, this alkaloid becomes injurious.

Only a small portion of fruit should be preserved at a time.

To keep jelly, there is no better way than to pour hot melted paraffin on top after the jelly has hardened, then adjust the covers. The old-fashioned way of cutting letter paper into circular pieces to just fit the tops of glasses, dipping them in alcohol or brandy and covering the jelly, putting on tin covers or circular pieces of paper cut larger than the glasses and fastening securely over the edges with mucilage or paste, is always good.

Iron or tin vessels should never be used in preparing fruits, as the action of the acids on the metals gives a dark color and disagreeable taste to the fruits. Preserving kettles should either be aluminum, porcelain-lined or the best granite ware. It is better to use a broad, open pan than a deep, narrow one, for the fruit should not be cooked in deep layers.

The perfect storing place for jellies and preserves requires three essentials: There must be coolness, dryness, and plenty of air circulation. Dryness without coolness is bad; coolness without dryness is injurious. As dryness in a house means some degree of warmth also, this cannot combine with a fair amount of coolness unless plenty of air be admitted.

In a cool, damp cupboard that is poorly ventilated, the preserves mold. In a warm atmosphere that is also damp, the preserves undergo the wine change. Sugars will combine with the fruit acids and evolve bubbles of carbonic acid, the familiar cause of fermentation. Alcohol will duly form, and the vinegar and vinous ferments will operate in turn. All the conditions for wine formation are in the preserve if it be not properly jellied or sufficiently boiled.

A storage place that is too warm will cause the sugar in preserves to undergo its crystalline change. Then the preserves will be full of hard, candied sugar of acid flavor, and the fruit will be withered and dry. Glass jars are now recognized as the ideal preserve jar, as they are not only air-tight, but also allow of inspection from time to time in order to detect incipient fermentation.

When making jellies avoid overdilution of juice; avoid an oversupply of sugar; avoid overcooking of juice and sugar together.

PRESERVING FRUIT BY DRYING

Preserving fruit by drying has its advantages in that an excess of fruit may be cared for in season when there is neither time nor room for cooking it. Also,

FOR LIFTING HOT JELLY JARS

7

Jellies, Jams and Preserves

its flavor being different from that of canned fruit, it affords an agreeable change from canned or jellied fruits.

Only sound, ripe fruit should be used for drying, and the process may be performed either by the sun or by artificial heat.

Where it can be accomplished without contamination by dust or flies, sun-drying seems to perfect the flavor of the product. On the other hand, fruit quickly dried by artificial heat better retains its color.

Sun-dried fruit should not be left out of doors over night, for dew will retard the process with no advantage to the fruit.

To prepare apples, pears, peaches, etc., for drying, wash and pare the fruit. Spread on wooden trays for sun-drying and on a wire rack if it is to be dried over a fire. When dry the fruit may be placed in muslin bags, and hung in a dry place.

Cherries, berries and other small fruits are prepared for evaporation thus: Use two cupfuls of sugar to each pound of fruit. Sprinkle enough sugar over the fruit to cover it, and let stand over night. Add a little water to the remainder of the sugar and in the morning boil the fruit in it for ten minutes. Take it out and drain. Reduce the syrup until it is quite thick, return the fruit to it and let it simmer at the back of the range for thirty minutes. Lay the fruit on buttered platters, and let it dry in the hot sun.

Apples, pears and peaches may also be dried in this way.

For evaporated melon, divide, pare and remove the cores of preserving citron melons. Cut the flesh into convenient pieces. Add one and one-half cupfuls of sugar to one pound of fruit; let stand over night under a weight to express the juice. In the morning drain off this syrup, and boil it for five minutes. Add the fruit, three grated lemons and two or three pieces of ginger root. Let cook until the fruit is clear and the syrup very thick. Remove to buttered platters, and dry for three days in the hot sun. When dry, pack it in glass jars, and cover tightly.

HOW TO DRY RASPBERRIES

Ripe black raspberries

Pick over the berries and toss them in clean towels to free them from dust. Spread them in layers, three berries deep, on fireproof plates. Place in the oven or on the back of the range until brought to scalding point, then remove to a place that is simply warm enough to keep the moisture slowly evaporating, but where there is no danger of burning. Stir occasionally with a wooden spoon.

In twelve or fourteen hours the fruit should be reduced to one-third its original bulk. It will take from thirty-six to forty-eight hours to remove all the moisture.

9

Jellies, Jams and Preserves

At the last the berries should be again brought to a scalding point, to insure freedom from insects. Cover in small cans or pails.

The berries should be washed in lukewarm water before using, and stewed in plenty of water, with sugar added just before serving.

TO DRY HERBS AND MUSHROOMS

Herbs   Mushrooms

Pull the herbs on a dry day, and just before they flower. Cut off the roots and free them from dust. Wash them thoroughly, then shake them, and spread them on a paper placed in a cool oven with the door open, or in the sun, until they are dry and crisp.

Strip the leaves from the stalks, crush them fine, or rub them through a coarse sieve. Place the powder in wide-mouthed bottles, cork securely, and label each one distinctly.

This conserves the flavor much more than if bunches of herbs are kept hanging up, even when they are protected from dust by being placed in paper bags.

Gather fresh mushrooms, free them from dust and decayed parts, then cut in thick slices, spread out on paper or plates, and place in a cool oven, or in the sun.

They may be pounded and rubbed through a sieve or they may be strung on a thread and dried in the sun. When perfectly dry put them in glass jars.

4

When wanted for use soak them for several hours in cold water and then use the same as fresh mushrooms.

AMBER MARMALADE

1 grape fruit	1 orange
1 lemon	Sugar

Shave the fruit very thin, rejecting the cores and the seeds.

Measure and add three times the quantity of water, then mix and allow to stand over night.

Boil it for fifteen minutes in the morning, then let stand for another night.

On the following morning add one pint of sugar for every pint of the mixture and boil steadily until it jellies. This usually takes about two hours.

Divide into glasses and cover with melted paraffin.

The sugar should be heated before it is added.

The difference between fruit marmalade and fruit butter is that the latter is fine and compact and is usually made by putting the fruit, after long cooking, through a sieve, while with marmalade the fruit is left in pieces.

APPLE JELLY

Apples	Sugar

Wash, core and cut up apples that are juicy and acid, but not too ripe. Put them into a preserving kettle with a small quantity of water, to keep them from burning. Keep covered; boil gently until quite soft, then strain through a jelly bag, measure the juice, then put it over the fire to boil.

Now take as many pints of sugar as of juice, and set it in the oven to heat, but not to get brown. The sugar is heated so that there will be no loss of time in the total cooking results. After the boiling has proceeded for twenty minutes, skim thoroughly and add the hot sugar. Stir gently, boil for five minutes more, skim if needed, and pour into sterilized glasses.

Cover with hot melted paraffin.

To make apple jelly in a fireless cooker, first wipe some apples, then remove all spots and cores. Put the cores and all good parings in the fireless aluminum kettle, and nearly cover them with cold water, then bring to the boil and boil for five minutes. Place at once in the fireless cooker and allow to remain over night; in the morning strain and make the jelly in the usual way. The apples may be canned.

To make apple jelly with cider, wash and dry tart apples, quarter and put into a preserving pan with cider to nearly cover. Cook slowly until the apples are nearly tender, then strain and measure the juice. Allow one pound of sugar for each two cupfuls of juice. Stir until the sugar is dissolved, remove the spoon and boil for five minutes longer. Pour into hot glasses and when cold cover with melted paraffin.

The paraffin must be very hot, not merely melted, that all germs that have fallen on the surface of the jelly may be killed and future trouble with them obviated.

To give variety to apple jelly the rose geranium will give a dainty flavor. Allow a clean, large leaf to two quarts, adding to the boiling juice a little before the sugar is put in. Remove in three or four minutes.

Two whole cloves to the same quantity of juice or a piece of stick cinnamon, about a finger long, will give apple jelly a piquant taste which will be liked.

Sprigs of mint may be used in the same way.

APPLE AND GRAPE BUTTER

10 lbs. apples	½ teaspoonful powdered ginger
7 lbs. grapes	
4 lbs. (8 cups) sugar	½ teaspoonful powdered mace
1 quart (4 cups) water	
1 teaspoonful powdered cinnamon	½ teaspoonful powdered cloves

Stem the grapes. Core and pare the apples and put them with the grapes and water into a saucepan. Boil until soft, strain through a sieve or press through a fruit press, add the sugar which has been heated and the spices. Cook and stir until thick.

Pour into jars and seal.

Jellies, Jams and Preserves

APPLE AND GRAPE JELLY

4 lbs. grapes   Sugar
14 apples

Boil the grapes and sliced apples until tender, then drain over night. In the morning measure, and to each cupful of juice allow one cupful of sugar.

Boil the juice for twenty minutes, then add the heated sugar and boil for fifteen minutes.

Pour into glasses and seal.

APPLE BUTTER

4 bushels apples	7 tablespoonfuls powdered cloves
10 gallons sweet cider	
13 lbs. brown sugar	14 tablespoonfuls powdered cinnamon
10 lbs. granulated sugar	
	1 teaspoonful grated nutmeg

Core and pare the apples, put them into a large pan with two quarts of water and begin to cook them. Add gradually the cider which has been boiled and skimmed. Boil, stirring constantly until it thickens, then stir in the sugar and the spices. Keep in a closely covered receptacle, and set in a cool, dark place.

Another Method: Cut sound apples, then boil them with a very little water, and strain as if making juice for a jelly. Take one gallon of this juice, and boil until it is reduced to half, then add two gallons of peeled and quartered apples and allow to cook to a mush. Now add one-half gallon of sugar, one teaspoonful of powdered allspice and one teaspoonful of grated nutmeg and cook for fifteen minutes longer. Remove from the fire and divide into sterilized jars and seal.

Apple butter may be made of sweet, or of half sweet and half sour apples.

Boil a gallon of fresh sweet cider down to half of its original quantity. Fill the preserving pan in which the cider was cooked with sliced apples, and pour cider over them. There should be enough cider to keep the apples from sticking to the pan. Simmer until thick as marmalade, then turn into stone jars and cover.

APPLE MARMALADE

8 lbs. apples	10 lbs. sugar
6 large lemons	2 quarts water

Slice the lemons, cover them with the water and let them stand over night. In the morning put them into a preserving pan, add the apples, peeled, cored and sliced, and boil for one hour. Then add the sugar, and boil for one and one-half hours longer.

Pour into glass jars and seal.

Another Method: Wipe six pounds of apples, pare and core them; put the skins and cores into a saucepan, cover with two cupfuls of cold water and boil

15

quickly for ten minutes. Drain away the juice, pressing the apple skins to get as much out of them as possible.

Grate the rinds of four lemons, adding four and one-half pounds of sugar. Now put the cut up apples into a wide jar, strain the lemon juice into the water in which the apple skins were boiled and pour over the sugar. Let it just melt and pour over the apples.

Cover the jar closely, and put it in the oven till the fruit is tender, then pour it into a saucepan and boil for three-fourths of an hour. Stir almost constantly, and when the mixture is coming away from the pan divide into small jars or cups. If these are brushed over with olive oil the marmalade will turn out whole.

One handful of blanched and shredded almonds added at the last gives the marmalade a nice appearance.

APRICOT AND ORANGE PRESERVE

9 lbs. ripe apricots	3 lbs. (6 cups) sugar
24 oranges	

Pare and slice the apricots, add the sugar, then the oranges peeled and shredded. The white of the orange peel should be removed. Allow the mixture to stand in a cool place for twenty-four hours.

Boil for thirty minutes, then seal in glass fruit jars.

Another Method: Peel four large, sweet seedless oranges, core with an apple corer and cut them into thin slices. Cover with boiling water and let stand over night.

At the same time put one pound of peeled dried apricots into a basin, add cold water to cover and let them soak over night. In the morning put the apricots and the oranges with their liquids into an agate pan and cook for one-half hour, then measure and add an equal quantity of sugar and boil until thick, stirring constantly.

Seal in glasses.

BANANA JAM

12 large bananas	4 lemons
6 oranges	Sugar

Large, coarse bananas, not too ripe, should be used, and the little slices should remain whole and present an inviting appearance. Cut the bananas, after peeling them, into rather thin, round slices.

To each pound of sliced bananas add three-fourths pound of sugar, the strained juice and pulp of the oranges and lemons.

Boil slowly for three-fourths of an hour. Seal in small glasses.

Another Method: Six pounds of bananas, two pounds of juicy pears, two lemons, four and one-half pounds of sugar. Cut the bananas up in small, equal sized pieces, and weigh. Put in the preserving pan the grated rinds and strained juice of the lemons, peeled pears cut up rather small, and one pound of the sugar. When boiling, put in gradually the bananas and the remaining sugar.

Stir the mixture gently till it boils. Boil fast for one hour.

Skim well, and pour into glasses or jars and seal.

BANANA MARMALADE

Bananas   Lemons
Sugar

Peel, and slice in rounds, ripe but firm bananas, and to every pound of the prepared fruit allow the grated rind and the strained juice of one lemon and one pound of lump sugar. Put all into an earthenware jar, cover and leave until the sugar is dissolved. Then pour into a preserving pan and bring gradually to the boil, stirring occasionally. Then boil rapidly, stirring all the time until it is thick.

Pour into jelly glasses and seal.

BARBERRIES IN MOLASSES

2 quarts barberries   1 quart molasses

Discard all imperfect berries and remove the stems. Put the molasses into a preserving pan, and when at the boiling point, pour in the berries. Boil them until rich and clear looking, stirring often lest the molasses burn.

Seal in jars.

BARBERRY JELLY

Barberries   Sugar

Gather the barberries as soon as they have been touched by the frost. Stem, wash, and to every four quarts allow one cupful of water. Cook until the juice presses out easily, remove from the fire, mash, strain and measure the juice.

To two cupfuls of juice allow two generous cupfuls of sugar. Place the sugar in the oven. Cook the juice for twenty minutes then add the sugar and cook for five minutes.

Divide into glasses and seal when cold.

BARBERRIES WITH APPLES

½ peck barberries   1 peck sweet apples
2 quarts molasses

Pick over the barberries, wash, and put on to boil with water enough to float them. Add the molasses and cook until the berries are tender. While they are cooking, pare, quarter, and core the apples.

Skim out the barberries and cook the apples in the syrup, as many as can be cooked conveniently. When tender, put them into a jar with the berries, and boil the syrup until it is thick.

Pour it over the fruit and the next morning heat all together again, and put away in a large stone jar.

Jellies, Jams and Preserves

Scald occasionally and the fruit will keep without sealing.

BLACKBERRY JELLY

Blackberries   Sugar

The uncultivated berry is the best for making jelly and should be rather underripe. Put the berries into a stone jar, stand in a pan of cold water, cover the top of the jar and boil slowly until the berries are quite soft. Now strain the juice, and to each pint allow one pound of sugar. Pour the juice into a porcelain-lined pan and boil for twenty minutes.

Heat the sugar, add it to the boiling juice, and stir until the sugar is thoroughly dissolved, then allow to boil again, pour into hot jelly glasses and seal.

Another Method: Instead of cooking the berries, put them through a food chopper, strain the juice and throw away the seeds, then boil the juice.

BLACK CURRANT JAM NO. 1

Black currants   Sugar
Rhubarb

Weigh and pick the currants and put them into a preserving pan, sprinkling with an equal weight of fine preserving sugar. Be careful when doing this to sprinkle the sugar in gradually in layers with the fruit, so as not to crush the latter. then leave them till the following day.

In the meantime take some more black currants, together with some peeled and sliced stalks of rhubarb, and cook till the juice has flowed freely ; then strain off all the liquid possible. Next take this juice, pour it over the sweetened currants, and let stand for twenty-four hours, allowing one cupful of juice to each pound of the preserved fruit. Now pour off all the juice which will have appeared, put it on to boil with an equal weight of sugar, allowing it to boil up rapidly, and, when it does, lay in the fruit, and boil for fifteen minutes, stirring it gently so as not to break the fruit, and removing every particle of scum as it rises.

Seal in glasses.

BLACK CURRANT JAM NO. 2

7 lbs. ripe black currants	1 gill (½ cup) water
7 lbs. (14 cups) sugar	1 tablespoonful butter

Strip the currants from their stalks, then weigh them and put into a preserving pan with the sugar and the water. Allow the pan to stand at the side of the fire until the sugar begins to dissolve, stirring occasionally. Now place the pan on the fire, again stir until all the sugar dissolves, and then allow the ingredients to boil for one-half hour.

The butter should be added when the jam comes to boiling point.

Test a little of the jam on a saucer, and, if it stiffens at once, pour into jars, cover when cold.

A USEFUL STAND AND JELLY BAG

Jellies, Jams and Preserves

The butter prevents the currants from becoming hard.

CARROT MARMALADE

1½ lbs. carrots	Sugar
2 lemons	

Wash and scrape the carrots, boil them until soft, then grind them through a food chopper.

Put the grated rinds and strained juice of the lemons into a saucepan and cook for five minutes. Measure the carrots, add them with an equal amount of sugar to the lemons, and cook for ten minutes. Seal in jelly glasses.

Another Method: Put into a preserving pan six cupfuls of grated carrots, six cupfuls of sugar, the grated rinds of two lemons, and the strained juice of six lemons and two oranges.

Cook slowly for two and one-half hours.

CHERRY CHEESE

Cherries	Sugar

Stone the cherries, then boil until soft. Press through a sieve or fruit press.

Weigh the pulp and boil it quickly to a dry paste, then stir in three-fourths cupful of sugar for every pound of fruit, and when this is thoroughly dissolved place the pan on the fire again and stir without ceasing until it is dry, and will not stick to the fingers when touched.

Press into glasses and cover with paraffin.

CHESTNUT JAM

Large chestnuts   Vanilla extract
Sugar

Boil some chestnuts in water; when tender, remove, peel, skin, and rub through a sieve while warm. Weigh this purée, and to every pound, allow the same quantity of sugar.

Put the purée and sugar into preserving pan and simmer for three-fourths of an hour, stirring all the time. Add vanilla extract to taste.

When cold, divide into small glasses and cover.

CITRON MELON CONSERVE

Citron melons   Ginger
Sugar   Alum

Peel small citron melons, slice, and cut into small pieces; cover with weak salt water, and stand over night; then soak in cold water for several hours; cover with fresh water, add a pinch of alum and boil until clear; drain, and when perfectly cold, to each pint of melon add two cupfuls of sugar and sufficient water to moisten it well; add a few pieces of ginger root; return to the fire, and simmer for two hours, when most of the sugar will have candied; pack in jars, and cover with the remaining syrup.

If a dry conserve is wished, place the citron on platters, and stand in the sunshine. When dried off, pack between layers of sugar.

It has been found that the citron melon contains a large proportion of pectin and it may be practically applied in "jelling" a number of other fruits that contain little pectin of their own.

COCOANUT JAM

2 large cocoanuts	¾ pint (1½ cups) water
½ lb. (1 cup) sugar	½ teaspoonful salt

Shell the cocoanuts and grate the meat, put it with the cocoanut liquid and one-half cupful of water into a saucepan and cook until soft.

Boil the sugar with one cupful of water and the salt for six minutes.

Add to the cocoanut and let the whole simmer for one hour.

Seal in glasses.

CRABAPPLE AND CRANBERRY JELLY

1 peck crabapples	1 quart cranberries
Sugar	

Cut the crabapples in small pieces without peeling or coring, add cold water even with the fruit and put over the fire in a porcelain-lined pan.

When about half done, add the well washed cranberries and cover. When quite soft turn into a jelly bag and let drip over night. Measure the liquid and provide an equal amount of sugar. Put the sugar into the oven, but do not let it burn.

Bring the liquid to boiling point, boil for twenty minutes, add the hot sugar, stir until dissolved, boil for three minutes and turn into glasses that have been standing in a pan of hot water.

Cover with melted paraffin.

The blending of these two fruits makes a most delicious product.

Another variation of crabapple jelly is obtained by proceeding in the same way, but omitting the cranberries. Let the sugar brown slightly in the oven before adding it to the apple juice.

After the juice has cooked for ten minutes, add the grated rind of one lemon, then add the sugar and allow to boil up for a moment. Pour into heated glasses and seal.

This jelly is of a beautiful amber color.

CRANBERRY MARMALADE

Cranberries	Carbonate of soda
Sugar	

It is not generally recognized that excellent tonic properties are contained in cranberries.

Pick over the cranberries, and to every quart of

fruit add two cupfuls of water and cook for one hour, stirring occasionally. Draw the saucepan to the side of the stove, and to every quart of the cranberries add one-half teaspoonful of carbonate of soda. Stir well, and carefully remove all scum as it rises. Then rub through a fine sieve, and to every cupful of the purée add one cupful of sugar.

Return to the pan and cook gently for thirty minutes. Divide into jars and seal.

CURRANT BAR-LE-DUC NO. 1

Currants   Sugar

Stem ripe currants, then weigh them, and allow two cupfuls of sugar to every pound of fruit.

Put the currants into a preserving pan, cover, heat slowly and cook gently for thirty minutes. Then add the sugar, previously heated, and shake the pan to mix, but do not stir. Watch very carefully, do not boil, but keep as hot as possible till the sugar is dissolved.

Divide into sterilized glasses and cover at once.

Red and white currants are beautiful preserved in this way.

CURRANT BAR-LE-DUC NO. 2

White or red currants   Sugar

Pick either white or red currants, but the white ones are preferable, and keep them in a cool place.

5

Weigh the currants before taking them off the stems and allow one cupful of sugar to a pound of fruit.

Put one-half cupful of water for each pound of sugar in the bottom of a porcelain-lined pan. Set the pan over a moderate fire and let the sugar boil gently to a thick syrup, stirring it frequently to keep it from sticking, and skimming it now and then.

In the meantime, pick one currant at a time off the stem. Take a slender needle which has been sharpened at one end, thrust it in the flower end of the currant, and push each seed out through the stem end. Save the juice which drops from the currants.

Drop the fruit into the syrup, a very few at a time. Just let them come to boiling point. Skim them out quickly onto a sieve, where they may drain for a few moments, then put them into small sterilized glasses, filling each glass with the fruit about one-fourth full. Now pour the juice into the pan and let it cook with the syrup, stirring it almost constantly till it jellies, then pour it hot over the fruit.

When it is firm, cover and seal the glasses.

Use the large cherry currants.

CURRANT JELLY

Currants · Sugar

Pick over the currants carefully but do not stem them, then wash and drain. Put them into a preserving kettle and set this in another larger vessel of hot water. As soon as the fruit begins to heat, mash with a potato masher or with a wooden pestle until reduced to a pulp.

Remove from the range and pour into a jelly bag to drain over night. Then measure out by pints and return to the kettle.

Take as many pounds of sugar as there are pints of juice and place on shallow tins in the oven to heat, taking care that they do not get hot enough to discolor the sugar.

Boil the juice for twenty minutes from the time it begins to boil, then add the heated sugar, stirring rapidly all the time. As soon as it is dissolved, remove the spoon, let it come to a boil again, then take at once from the fire and pour into hot jelly glasses.

Cover with melted paraffin.

When white currants are used for jelly, less sugar will be required; three-fourths of a pound of sugar sufficing for one pint of juice.

Be sure that the currants are dry when gathered and not overripe.

GOLDEN MARMALADE

5 navel oranges	Sugar
2 lemons	Water

Cut off the ends of the oranges; quarter them and slice as thin as possible. Cut up one of the lemons in the same manner, rejecting the seeds, and add to the oranges.

Measure the sliced fruit and to every two cupfuls of it add three cupfuls of cold water; let it stand uncovered in a cool place for twenty-four hours. Then put it into a graniteware pan and allow it to boil without sugar for forty-five minutes. Add the strained juice of the second lemon, measure, and to every two cupfuls add three cupfuls of sugar.

Boil for forty-five minutes, and be careful that it does not burn.

Pour into glasses and allow to cool.

Cover with melted paraffin and lids or paper.

PEAR AND PINEAPPLE MARMALADE

4 quarts pears   4 lbs. (8 cups) sugar
2 large pineapples

Pare, core and quarter the pears; pare the pineapples and carefully remove the eyes.

Put them through a food chopper into a porcelain-lined pan, add the sugar and boil until clear.

Seal in glasses.

CURRANT AND CHERRY PRESERVE

3 quarts currants   8 lbs. (16 cups) sugar
12 quarts cherries

Wash and stem the currants, then put them into a preserving kettle and cook until the juice begins to exude. Crush and strain to get out all the juice.

Jellies, Jams and Preserves

Stone the cherries and put them into a preserving pan, add the currant juice and the sugar.

Heat very slowly to boiling point, skim and then simmer for fifteen minutes.

Seal in small glasses.

CURRANT MARMALADE

Red or black currants   Sugar

Currant marmalade may be made of either ripe red or black currants. Strip them from the stems, wash and drain, then put in a kettle and cook and mash. Rub through a fine sieve that will prevent the seeds from going through. For every pound of the pulp allow one pound of sugar for red currants, or three-fourths pound of sugar for black or white currants.

Cook the pulp for twenty-five minutes, add the sugar, stir and cook until a little put on a cool saucer retains its shape and does not spread.

Put into jars and cover when cool.

DAMSON CHEESE

Ripe damsons   Sugar

Wash the damsons, put them into an earthenware jar, cover closely, place the jar in a pan of cold water on the fire and boil until the damsons are tender.

Skin and stone them, then rub through a sieve back into the juice which has been put into a preserving pan, add one cupful of sugar and a few of the kernels blanched to every pound of pulp, boil quickly to a stiff paste, continue boiling and stirring well until it leaves the pan dry, and adheres to the spoon in a mass; if it does not stick to the fingers when lightly touched it is cooked sufficiently.

Press it quickly into sterilized jars and cover with melted paraffin.

This is an old English preserve made much stiffer than either jelly or jam.

DAMSON JELLY

7 lbs. damsons   Sugar

Wipe the damsons with a damp cloth, place them in a preserving pan, and just cover with cold water. Boil for one-half hour or until soft. Pour through a jelly bag and then measure the juice.

To every two cupfuls of juice allow two cupfuls of sugar.

Put the juice and the sugar into a preserving pan and allow to boil for fifteen minutes.

Equal quantities of damsons and apples make a delightful variety of this jelly. The apples are merely wiped, the skins being kept on when fruit is cut into slices. The jelly is then made in the same way as the damson preserve.

Seal in jelly glasses.

Jellies, Jams and Preserves

DATE MARMALADE

3 lbs. stoned dates	1 lb. (2 cups) sugar
1 lb. dried apples	1½ pints (3 cups) water

Wash the apples and soak them over night in water; next morning drain, cut them into small pieces, and mix with dates. Add sugar and water, and boil thirty minutes.

Seal in glasses.

Another Method: Stone two and one-half pounds of dates, add six cupfuls of water and simmer until dates are soft. Add one pound of sugar and mix well. Remove from fire and add one-half pound of chopped English walnut meats.

ELDERBERRY JAM

1 lb. elderberries	¾ lb. sugar

Remove the stems from some elderberries, then weigh them, add the sugar, and cook until almost thick.

The mixture must not be too stiff. Divide into glasses and seal.

Another Method: Strip ripe fruit from the stalks, and boil with a little water for fifteen minutes, having taken care to weigh the fruit.

To six pounds of the berries allow four pounds of sugar. Boil for fifteen minutes, then add one tablespoonful of orange flower water and boil for three-fourths of an hour.

Seal in glasses.

FIG JAM

1 lb. figs	⅛ teaspoonful powdered
2½ lbs. apples	cinnamon
1 lemon	⅛ teaspoonful grated nut-
½ lb. (1 cup) sugar	meg
	1 quart water
	7 cloves

Grind figs in food chopper. Core, pare and chop the apples, and put into a saucepan with the figs, grated lemon rind and strained juice, spices and water. When half done add the heated sugar.

Seal in jars.

Another Method: Wash one pound of figs, cut them into quarters and put them in a saucepan with one pint of cold water. Boil slowly for two hours, and pour into a dish to get cold. Take four pounds of apples, wash them, cut them into rough pieces, put them into a clean saucepan, with five cupfuls of water, boil for one and one-half hours, then strain without pressure through a jelly bag.

Put the juice into a preserving kettle, add the figs and allow to boil for fifteen minutes, then add four pounds of heated sugar, eight pieces of whole ginger, and boil until it sets.

Jellies, Jams and Preserves

FIG PRESERVE

Ripe figs   Sugar

Gather the figs when fully ripe, but not cracked open; place them in a wire basket, and dip for a moment into a kettle of hot and moderately strong lye, or if preferred let them lie an hour in lime water and afterward drain. Make a syrup in the proportion of one pound of sugar to one pound of fruit, let the sugar dissolve, then boil it quickly for five minutes with lid off the pan, keeping it well skimmed. When the figs are drained add them to the hot syrup and cook well, then remove, boil down the syrup, leaving only enough to cover the fruit. Boil all together for one minute and seal while hot in glass jars.

Store in a cool, dry place.

Another Method: Either steam the figs, or simmer them gently so as not to break them, until they are almost transparent. Then take them from the steamer or take them from their liquid onto a platter and make a heavy syrup, using their own liquor as far as possible. When the syrup is very thick put the figs back into it carefully, and boil gently for ten minutes. Again skim the fruit out and pack into wide-mouthed jars, filling them not more than two-thirds full. The fruit will settle at first, but will float again as the jar is filled with syrup.

Seal at once.

FOUR-FRUIT JAM

2 quarts stoned cherries	1 pint raspberries
1 quart currants	Sugar
1 quart gooseberries	

"Top and tail" the gooseberries, pick the raspberries, currants, and cherries, and weigh three-fourths of a pound of sugar to every pound of fruit. Put the fruit and the sugar into a preserving pan and boil until thick.

Cover and seal in glasses.

FOUR-FRUIT JELLY

Cherries	Raspberries
Gooseberries	Sugar
Strawberries	

Pick the strawberries and raspberries, stone and stem the cherries and "top and tail" the gooseberries. Take equal quantity of these fruits and crush them under heavy pressure or put them through a fruit press, then strain the juice.

Strain the juice again into a preserving pan and boil it for twenty minutes. Allow three-fourths of a pound of sugar to each pint of liquid.

Heat the sugar, then add it and boil for five minutes. Seal in glasses.

Jellies, Jams and Preserves

GINGER APPLES

3 quarts sour, smooth skinned apples

3 quarts sugar

1 pint (2 cups) water

2 ozs. white ginger root

Pinch red pepper

Pound or grind the ginger root through a food chopper, put it into a porcelain-lined saucepan, add the red pepper, water and sugar. Now core, pare and chop the apples, add them, and cook until the fruit is transparent.

Seal in glass jars.

GINGER CONSERVE

¼ lb. ginger root

1 lb. (2 cups) sugar

½ pint (1 cup) water

Boil the sugar and water together until the syrup spins a heavy thread. Cut the ginger root into small pieces, boil in water for one hour, drain, cover with some of the syrup and boil slowly for one and one-half hours. Take up, drain, and when cold, dust with sugar; dip again into the syrup, cool, roll well in sugar and pack in jars, with sugar sprinkled between the layers.

Seal.

GINGER PEARS

8 lbs. pears

6 lbs. sugar

1 lb. preserved ginger

4 lemons

Wash the lemons, then put them into a saucepan with cold water to cover, and boil for one hour.

Peel, core and slice the pears, add the ginger, cut in small pieces, and cook with the sugar for one hour, stirring occasionally.

Drain, slice, and seed the lemons, then add them to the pear mixture, and continue to boil for one hour longer.

Divide into glass jars and seal.

GOOSEBERRY AND PINEAPPLE JAM

5 quarts gooseberries   Sugar
1 large pineapple

Pare and chop the pineapple, and "top and tail" the gooseberries. Measure three-fourths of a quart of sugar to each quart of fruit. Put the sugar into a porcelain-lined kettle with one cupful of water and let it boil and clarify. Now add the fruit and cook until thick.

GRAPE AND PEAR MARMALADE

Grapes   Sugar
Pears

Use equal weights of ripe grapes and pears. Pick and wash the grapes, then cook them in a little water until soft, and press them through a colander or fruit press. Add the pears, peeled, cored, and sliced, and simmer until thickened.

For Grape Jelly

39

Jellies, Jams and Preserves

Use a wooden spoon or paddle for stirring and keep an asbestos mat under the preserving pan to prevent burning. Sweeten to taste, and pack in jars.

GRAPE BAR-LE-DUC

Green grapes   Sugar

Wash and dry green grapes, then cut them in halves and remove the seeds. Weigh the grapes and to each pound allow one pound of sugar. Put the grapes into a preserving pan with enough water to come half the depth of the fruit. Heat slowly and when near the boiling point sprinkle in the sugar, a little at a time, adding more as it melts. When a syrup is formed, skim and simmer, until a little dropped on a saucer forms a jelly.

Stir as little as possible, in order to keep the shape of the grapes, and if the cooking is done slowly, and care taken that it does not scorch on the bottom of the pan, there will be little need of stirring.

Seal in small glasses.

GRAPE FRUIT MARMALADE

4 grape fruit   6 lemons
6 oranges   Sugar

Cook the grape fruit and the oranges separately in water to cover them, until soft enough to be easily pierced with a fork. Leave over night in the water in which they have been boiled. In the morning cut the grape fruit in halves, scoop out the pulp and press through a colander or fruit press to remove the seeds and tough core. Shred the rinds fine with a sharp knife.

Cut the oranges in slices, saving the juice from both fruits. To the shaved skins and pulp allow two quarts of cold water. Now measure and add one and one-half times the quantity of sugar, having both the sugar and juice hot. Add the strained lemon juice, then cook gently until thick.

Pour into sterilized glasses, but do not seal down for a day.

GRAPE JELLY

Fresh picked grapes   Sugar

For this grape jelly use ripe Concord, Isabella or Clinton grapes. Put the grapes into a large earthenware jar, stand it in a large saucepan of cold water, cover the top, and heat slowly until the fruit is soft. Now put a small quantity at a time into a jelly bag or fruit press and squeeze out all the juice. Measure the juice and to each pint allow two cupfuls of sugar.

Pour the juice into a porcelain-lined pan and stand it over a quick fire. Put the sugar into fireproof dishes and place it in the oven to heat. Boil the juice rapidly for twenty minutes, then turn in the sugar, stirring briskly all the while until the sugar is dissolved.

Jellies, Jams and Preserves

Watch the liquid carefully and as soon as it comes to a boil remove from the fire and pour into sterilized tumblers.

If the fruit is overripe it will never jelly, no matter how long it is boiled.

Another Method: To one gallon of grapes, green or ripe, picked and washed and thoroughly drained of all water; add one-half cupful of water and cook until the fruit is thoroughly done, do not stir but keep pushed down in the juice.

Strain; and to each pound of juice add one pound of sugar, while the juice is very hot. Stir until all the sugar is dissolved and pour into glasses.

Seal when cold.

GRAPE MARMALADE
1 gallon stemmed green grapes   Sugar

Stem and wash the grapes, then drain them and put them into a preserving pan with two cupfuls of water. Cook until soft, rub through a sieve, or force through a fruit press and add an equal amount of sugar to the pulp.

Boil hard for twenty-five minutes, taking care that it does not burn, then pour into glasses.

Cover with melted paraffin.

GREENGAGE JAM
6 lbs. greengages   4 lbs. lump sugar

Skin and stone ripe greengages, boil them quickly

for three-fourths of an hour, with a little sugar, keeping them stirred constantly; then add four pounds of pounded lump sugar to six pounds of ripe greengages. Boil the fruit for ten minutes longer, skimming it frequently as the scum rises.

Pour into glasses and seal.

Another Method: Firm, sound greengages are required for this preserve. Wipe seven pounds of the fruit, remove the stalks and stones and crack a few of the latter, placing the kernels to one side. Then blanch the kernels.

Put the prepared fruit and the kernels into a preserving pan and add cold water to the depth of one inch. Bring to boiling point and boil for ten minutes. Now add seven pounds of heated sugar, stirring all the time.

Boil the preserve rapidly for twenty minutes, then pour into glasses and seal.

GREENGAGE PRESERVE

Greengages   Sugar

Wipe the fruit, and prick the skins with a needle. Put the fruit into a preserving pan with just enough water to cover, set over a gentle fire until it begins to simmer, then skim out the fruit, putting it on a sieve to drain. Add three pounds of sugar to the water in which the greengages were boiled; boil quickly, skimming until the syrup sticks to the spoon; now

Jellies, Jams and Preserves

put in the fruit and boil until the syrup bubbles, then
pour it all in a large bowl and allow to stand over
night.

Drain the syrup from the fruit, let it boil up quickly,
pour it over the fruit again, and stand another day,
then boil all together for six minutes; pour into jars
and seal.

GREEN TOMATO BUTTER

9 lbs. green tomatoes	3 tablespoonfuls powdered
1 pint (2 cups) vinegar	cinnamon
1 tablespoonful powdered	1½ tablespoonfuls pow-
cloves	dered allspice
	½ teaspoonful salt

Wash and dry the tomatoes, then cut out the stem
ends but do not peel them. Slice them fine into an
enameled pan, then add the vinegar, salt and spices
and boil for four hours or until quite thick.

The butter should be stirred often to prevent
burning.

Seal in jars.

GREEN TOMATO PRESERVE

12 lbs. green tomatoes	4 lemons
9 lbs. lump sugar	3 ozs. ginger root
¼ lb. candied citron peel	¼ oz. chilies

Wipe the tomatoes, cut them in quarters, place
them in a large preserving pan, add the sugar, the

6

grated rinds and the strained juice of lemons and let stand for twenty-four hours.

Bruise the ginger, then tie it in a small bag with the chilies, add them to the tomatoes and boil for one and one-half hours or until tender.

Just before the boiling is finished, remove the spice bag and add the peel cut into thin strips.

Divide into jars and seal.

LEMON MARMALADE

3 lbs. lemons   Sugar
3½ pints (7 cups) water

Wash the lemons, then pare them and cut the peel into very slender chips. Put the chips in a small saucepan, with two cupfuls of the water, and boil for forty minutes. Now take all the white part from the lemons and cut up the pulp roughly, put it into a preserving pan, with the remainder of the water, and boil one and one-quarter hours. This is counted after it begins to boil. Stir it frequently; then strain it through a jelly bag without pressure. Add the skins and the liquid with them. Now measure the liquid, and for each cupful allow two cupfuls of sugar.

Return to the pan and boil for thirty minutes.

Put into jars and cover for use.

LOGANBERRY JAM

Loganberries   Sugar

Crush some loganberries thoroughly, heat them in a

covered kettle, then simmer gently for thirty minutes. Add one pound of sugar for every pound of fruit, and boil for another thirty minutes.

Loganberries with strawberries are delicious. Take equal quantities of the fruits, then weigh them. Take one pound of sugar for every pound of mixed fruit, and proceed as with the above jam.

Pour into glasses and cover with melted paraffin.

'MATRIMONY JAM

2 lbs. apples	2 lbs. pears
2 lbs. plums	5½ lbs. (11 cups) sugar

Pare and core the apples, and stone the plums. Put the stones of the plums and the parings of the apples into a preserving pan with two cupfuls of water. Simmer for thirty minutes and strain.

While this is cooking peel and core the pears. Cut the apples and pears, and have them ready.

Put the strained juice in the preserving pan with the sugar, and when it boils, put in the apples, pears and plums.

Boil for thirty minutes, then pour into glasses and cover.

MEDLEY PRESERVE

1 quart red raspberries	2 large oranges
1 quart red currants	1 lb. sultana raisins
1 quart red cherries	Sugar
1 ripe pineapple	

Wash and stone the cherries, pick and wash the raspberries, stem the currants, pare and shred the pineapple and cut the oranges into small pieces without skinning them. Wash and dry the raisins.

Measure the fruit, put it into a preserving pan over a slow fire and simmer for one hour, stirring often.

Heat as many pounds of sugar as there are pounds of fruit, add to the boiling fruit, and cook to the consistency of marmalade.

Seal in jars.

MINT AND RHUBARB CONSERVE

1 quart chopped mint	1 quart (4 cups) sugar
1½ quarts rhubarb	

Wash and dry the rhubarb and cut it into small pieces, then put it into a preserving pan with the sugar and the mint. Cook until thick and put into small jars.

Cover when cold. Serve with meats.

MORELLO CHERRY PRESERVE

Morello cherries	½ pint (1 cup) currant
Lump sugar	juice

Pick the cherries when ripe, stem but do not pit. Prick each one with a needle to prevent bursting. For each pound of cherries allow one and one-half pounds of sugar. Roll and crush part of the sugar, sprinkle it over the cherries and let them stand over night.

Jellies, Jams and Preserves

In the morning dissolve the rest of the sugar in the currant juice, in a preserving pan over a slow fire. Add the cherries and simmer until they are tender but not broken.

Put the cherries into glasses or jars, boil the syrup until thick, then pour it over the fruit and seal.

MOUNTAIN ASH BERRY JELLY

Ripe mountain ash berries	Water
Sugar	Blackberry juice

Rinse and stem the berries, put them into a preserving pan with just enough water to cover. Boil until soft, strain through a bag or sieve, then put into the pan with one pound of lump sugar to each pint of juice. Boil quickly for thirty minutes, skimming carefully. A little blackberry juice added just before the jelly is ready gives a nice flavor.

Divide into glasses and cover.

Another Method: Strip ripe red mountain ash berries from their stalks, then wash them and put them into a preserving pan, with sufficient water to prevent their burning. Allow one cupful of water to every two pounds of fruit, and simmer, stirring and breaking the berries with a wooden spoon to make the juice flow. When quite soft, turn them into a jelly bag, and allow to run slowly, without squeezing. Weigh the juice, and return it to the pan, with two pounds of heated sugar to each two cupfuls of juice, and boil until it "jells."

Seal in glasses.

MULBERRY JELLY

Unripe mulberries   Sugar

Use only hard, unripe mulberries, and put these into the preserving pan in the proportions of two pints of cold water to six pints of berries. Let the fruit cook slowly for one hour, then add another quart of cold water, and simmer for another hour. Strain off the juice, and add one pound of heated sugar to each pint of mulberry juice.

Boil up again, and strain into glasses.

Cover with paraffin.

MULBERRY MARMALADE

Mulberries   Sugar

Free the berries from stalks and then weigh. For every pound take the same quantity of crushed lump sugar. Arrange the fruit at the bottom of a large flat preserving pan, and then sprinkle the sugar over it. Place the pan over a very slow fire, and cook until a thick syrup is formed, then boil quickly for a few minutes, removing the scum.

Pour into jelly glasses and seal.

Jellies, Jams and Preserves

MUSK-MELON BUTTER

12 musk-melons　　　　　　　Powdered cinnamon
Sugar

Wash, peel and seed the melons, then cut them into small pieces and put them into a large porcelain-lined pan. Cover them with cold water and boil until tender.

Drain, then rub them through a colander or fruit press. Measure the purée, add half as much sugar, and cook to a thick butter.

Flavor with powdered cinnamon to taste. A few chopped nut meats may be added, if liked.

Seal in jars.

MUSK-MELON PRESERVE

1 musk-melon
½ lemon
2 sour apples
2 rose geranium leaves
¼ teaspoonful ground cassia buds

⅛ teaspoonful ground cloves
1 tablespoonful chopped preserved ginger
Sugar

Pare the melon, cut it into small pieces and then weigh. Cut the lemon into thin pieces and put it into the preserving pan, then put in the melon, cover with cold water, and stew until tender.

Add the apples pared and cut into small pieces, the spices, geranium leaves and two-thirds the weight of the melon in sugar.   Boil quickly until the pieces of melon are transparent.   Remove the geranium leaves when they begin to fall to pieces.

Seal, while hot, in jars.

ORANGE AND GRAPE JAM

6 oranges	4 lbs. (8 cups) sugar
2 lbs. seeded raisins	6 lbs. ripe grapes

Cut off the thin rinds from the oranges and chop with the raisins.   Skin and seed the grapes and then cook until tender, add the skins, cook for fifteen minutes, add sugar, raisins, orange peel, and strained juice from the oranges.

Cook gently until thick, then seal in jars.

ORANGE AND PEACH JAM

4 oranges	1½ lbs. peaches
Sugar	

Peel, remove seeds and white portions from the oranges, then nearly cover with boiling water and allow to stand over night.

Wash the peaches, nearly cover with boiling water, and allow to stand over night.   In the morning remove the skins and pits.

Put the oranges and the peaches, with the liquor from both, in a preserving pan, and cook for thirty minutes.   Then add an equal quantity of heated sugar and boil until thick, stirring frequently.

Pour into glasses and seal.

Jellies, Jams and Preserves

ORANGE AND PINEAPPLE MARMALADE

6 oranges	4 lbs. (8 cups) sugar
2 pineapples	1½ quarts water

Wash the oranges and soak them in the water over night. Boil them in the same water in the morning until tender, then cut them into small pieces, return them to the pan with the sugar and the pineapples cut fine. Boil the mixture, stirring all the time, until it jellies.

Canned pineapple may be used if the fresh cannot be obtained.

Other Methods: Pare, remove the eyes, then grate the pineapples, preserving the juice. Allow three-fourths of a pound of sugar to each pound of grated fruit. Boil till it jellies, pour into glass jars and seal.

Peel and grate or chop as many pineapples as desired, using a silver fork or knife in the operation. Measure or weigh and allow one pound of sugar to each pound of fruit. Mix well and stand in a cool place over night. In the morning cook one-half hour or until soft enough to put through a coarse sieve. Strain, return to the pan and continue cooking, stirring constantly for one-half hour or longer, until it is a clear amber jelly that will thicken into a paste as it cools.

Put into small jars and seal when cool.

ORANGE JELLY

2 sweet oranges	1 lemon
10 bitter oranges	Sugar

Wash and wipe the fruit, then cut it up roughly into a basin. Cover with ten quarts of cold water and allow to stand for twenty-four hours. Then boil gently for four hours, and strain over night through a jelly bag. Measure the juice and allow one pound of sugar to each pint of juice. Boil the juice for twenty minutes, then add the sugar which should have been heated and boil briskly for ten minutes.

Pour into jelly glasses and seal.

Another Method: Wash, wipe and grate ten bitter oranges, two sweet oranges and one lemon, cut up roughly into a basin, and put into a preserving pan with just enough cold water to cover and float the fruit from the bottom of the pan. Put on the fire and boil gently for two and one-half hours. Press through a fine sieve or through a fruit press. Measure the juice and allow one pound of sugar for each pint of juice.

Boil the juice and the sugar which has been heated for a few minutes, pour into glasses, and seal.

ORANGE MARMALADE

6 bitter oranges	6 pints (12 cups) water
2 sweet oranges	Sugar
2 lemons	

Jellies, Jams and Preserves

Wash and dry the oranges and lemons, then cut them into very small pieces, rejecting the seeds. Pour the water over the fruit and allow to stand for twenty-four hours. Boil until tender and let stand for another twenty-four hours. Now measure, and to each pint add two cupfuls of sugar. Boil until clear.

Seal in glasses.

Another Method: Take twelve oranges, three lemons, eight pounds of sugar and three quarts of water. Wash and dry the fruit, then slice it very thin, cutting each slice into four pieces. Reject all the seeds. Pour the water over the fruit and let it stand for twenty-four hours, then boil for two or three hours or until tender. Now add the sugar and boil for one-half hour longer.

Divide into glasses, cover with melted paraffin and seal.

ORANGE MARMALADE WITH HONEY

12 large ripe bitter oranges   Sugar
Honey

Cut the oranges into quarters, remove the rinds, seeds, and all the white pith, but be careful to save the juice. Put the pulp and the juice into a porcelain-lined pan with an equal weight of strained honey, and one-third as much sugar as honey; boil until very thick, sweet, and clear.

PARSLEY JELLY

Parsley   Sugar

Take a quantity of fresh parsley, wash, put in a preserving kettle, and press it down. Cover with cold water, boil gently for thirty minutes, then pour through a jelly bag twice.

Measure the juice and for every pint allow three-fourths of a pound of sugar. Boil the juice for twenty minutes, then add the heated sugar and boil for ten minutes.

Pour into glasses and seal.

PEACH BUTTER

2 lbs. dried peaches   1½ pints sugar
1 can peaches

Cook the dried peaches until tender, mash, rub through a sieve, or press through fruit press; also press through the can of peaches, add the sugar and cook slowly for two hours, being careful that it does not burn.

Pour into sterilized jars and seal.

PEACH JELLY

Peaches   Lemons
Sugar

For peach jelly select peaches not quite ripe enough for eating. Rub off the down with a rough cloth, cut in pieces, saving the pits. Cover with water and

Jellies, Jams and Preserves

cook slowly, closely covered, until the fruit is quite soft. Pour into a jelly bag and allow to drip.

When all the juice is extracted, measure, and to every two cupfuls of juice, allow one pound of sugar and the strained juice of one lemon.

Set the sugar in the oven to heat, and place the juice uncovered over the fire. Cook for twenty minutes, add the heated sugar, stir until dissolved, cook for five minutes, then strain into glasses and cover when cold.

Peaches never make a firm jelly that will retain its shape when turned from a mold or glass, but no jelly is more delicious for cake fillings, sauces, puddings or candies.

Another Method: Wash one peck of peaches and wipe them dry. Cut into pieces without peeling, and discard all the pits but eight. Crush these and add to the fruit. Place in the preserving pan, add one quart of water, and cook until tender. Drain, boil syrup again for fifteen minutes, strain and add one tablespoonful of lemon juice for each two cupfuls of juice and an equal amount of heated sugar, then allow to cook for ten minutes.

Test and see if it will jelly; if not, boil two or three minutes longer.

PEAR AND BARBERRY PRESERVES

Barberries   Sugar
Pears

Free the barberries from the stems, then weigh them, and make a syrup with the same amount of sugar, allowing one cupful of water to two cupfuls of sugar.

When the syrup is clear put in the barberries and boil for fifty minutes; as soon as the barberries are cooked take them out with a skimmer. Now put as many peeled and quartered pears as there are barberries into the syrup and boil until tender, then take them out and mix with the barberries.

Boil the syrup for thirty minutes longer and pour immediately over the fruit.

Seal.

PEAR AND CRANBERRY MARMALADE

4 quarts pears	4 lbs. (8 cups) brown sugar
2 quarts cranberries	

Put the sugar into a preserving pan, add the pears, cored and peeled, and cook until half done, then add the cranberries and cook until thick. This will require twenty minutes.

PINEAPPLE AND APRICOT MARMALADE

4 lbs. apricots	Sugar
1 large pineapple	

Wash the apricots well, but do not peel them. Break them in halves, saving ten of the kernels.

Jellies, Jams and Preserves

Peel and shred the pineapple, put it into a saucepan and place over a slow fire. When it reaches boiling point, add the apricots and the seed kernels.

Boil very slowly for about one hour, then weigh. Add an equal amount of heated sugar and continue to cook slowly until thick.

Pour into heated glasses, and when cold cover with melted paraffin and lids.

Another Method: Scald and peel ten pounds of apricots, then boil them in their own juice for three-fourths of an hour, add seven pounds of sugar and boil for ten minutes; then add one can of pineapple cut in small pieces, and the strained juice of four lemons, and boil for ten minutes; add one-half cupful of blanched almonds and three blanched and chopped apricot kernels.

PINEAPPLE AND STRAWBERRY CONSERVE

Fresh pineapples   Sugar
Ripe strawberries

Pare and remove the eyes from perfectly ripe, sound pineapples. Cut the pineapples into small pieces and mix them with an equal amount of hulled ripe strawberries. Now add as much sugar as there is fruit and cook until very thick, stirring now and then to prevent burning.

Seal in small glasses.

PINEAPPLE AND VEGETABLE MARROW JAM

1 can or 1 fresh pineapple Sugar
Vegetable marrows   Salt

Cut and peel the vegetable marrows, weigh and put into salt water, allowing two tablespoonfuls of salt to one gallon of water, then set in a cool place over night.

Drain, dry them, and cut into pieces about two inches square. Place these in a large earthenware dish, and to each pound of marrow allow three-fourths of a pound of sugar and to three pounds of marrow allow one can of pineapple cut into squares.

Add the pineapple juice and leave for twenty-four hours. Boil till clear. This takes about two hours.

Seal in jars.

PINEAPPLE CONSERVE

Sugar-loaf pineapples   Sugar

Peel the pineapples, remove the eyes, and cut into thick slices, up and down instead of across, in order not to use the hard core; scald in clear water until tender, then add two-thirds cupful of sugar to each cupful of the water in which it was scalded, return to the fire, and when the syrup is cooked down thick, add the fruit, and cook for thirty minutes; pack in jars, and cover with the syrup.

When ready to use, if preferred dry, drain and roll in sugar.

Fruits for conserves should always be just ripe

Jellies, Jams and Preserves

and of the best quality; use porcelain-lined pans in
their preparation, and either silver or wooden spoons.
Granulated sugar is the best for all conserves.

PLUM, APPLE AND PEAR MARMALADE

Plums   Pears
Apples   Sugar

Scald the plums and peel them, cut in two and remove the stones. Then pack in layers alternately
with peeled and sliced apples and pears, adding as
much sugar as there is of fruit.

Set on the back of the range, and cook very slowly
until smooth and thick.

Seal in jars.

PLUM JELLY

Plums   Sugar

Wash and drain the plums, put them in a preserving
kettle with just enough cold water to cover them, and
let them boil until quite tender, then drain, but do
not squeeze, or the jelly will not be clear.

Measure the juice and put it on to boil, put the
same amount of sugar in shallow pans in the oven
to heat, and when the juice has boiled for twenty
minutes, stir in the hot sugar. When the juice boils
again pour into scalded jelly glasses set in a dish of
hot water.

Seal while hot.

7

PRESERVED CANTALOUPES

Yellow cantaloupes or musk-   Sugar
    melons   Water

Select the large yellow variety of cantaloupe or the old-fashioned muskmelons when they are beginning to turn a little yellow in ripening. Peel the thin outer rind, and cut a very thin slice next the seeds; cut the sections in pieces one inch thick, and put them into a preserving pan with six pounds of sugar to ten pounds of fruit. Add one-half gallon of water, cover and boil until the melon becomes clear and transparent.

Remove the cover and boil until the syrup is thick. Seal in jars.

PRESERVED CHERRIES

Morello cherries   Sugar

Stone the cherries, and if morello or pie cherries are used, allow one cupful of sugar to every pound of fruit; if ox-hearts, one-half cupful of sugar to every pound of fruit.

Put the cherries into a preserving kettle, cover them with the sugar and let them stand for two hours, then place over a moderate fire and bring to boiling point.

Skim and seal in jars.

Another Method: Wipe and stone some cherries,

Jellies, Jams and Preserves

then cover them with vinegar and allow them to stand over night in a cool place. Next day drain off the vinegar and cherry juice. Put the cherries into a stone crock with alternate layers of sugar, allowing three-fourths of a pound of sugar for every pint of cherries. Cover and keep in a cool place.

Stir with a wooden spoon, gently, so as not to break the fruit, every day for ten days.

Seal in small jars.

The vinegar and cherry juice may be boiled with sugar for a beverage.

PRESERVED CITRON MELONS

Citron melons	Seeded raisins
Ginger root	Lemons
Sugar	

Peel off the green rind of the melons, cut them in halves and remove the soft centers. Then cut the fruit into diamonds, strips, or any fancy shapes preferred.

Weigh, and for each six pounds of the prepared fruit allow one quart of water and one-fourth pound of ginger root.

Clean and scrape the root, put all into a preserving kettle and place at the back of the stove, where the mixture will simmer for one and one-half hours.

Meantime make a syrup, using five pounds of sugar for every six pounds of fruit and adding two cupfuls of water to the sugar. Remove the ginger root from the citron and, when the sugar is dissolved, pour the syrup over the citron and cook for one-half hour longer. Then skim out the fruit and spread on a platter, letting it stand in the sunshine or in the oven while the raisins and lemons are added to the syrup. Use three lemons and one pound of raisins. The lemons should be sliced thin and the seeds rejected. Cook until a rich, thick syrup results. Return the melon to the syrup, cook for fifteen minutes longer, then divide into jars and seal.

Melon preserve is usually made with the melon cut in dice, but it is far more delicious when grated, and the syrup and flavorings penetrate quicker. Cook the grated citron melon in a rich syrup flavored with grated lemon rind and strained lemon juice. One-half lemon to two cupfuls of sugar is a good allowance.

PRESERVED CUCUMBERS

3 large cucumbers	Lemons
Sugar	Whole ginger
Water	

Wash the cucumbers, put them into a strong brine, cover, and set aside for five days. Drain and wash in cold water and put them into a saucepan, cover with salted water, put on the lid, and allow to stand over a slow fire until the cucumbers are thoroughly green, then remove from the fire and let stay in the pan until cold.

Jellies, Jams and Preserves

Quarter each cucumber, remove all the pulp and seeds, and allow the pieces to stand in a pan of cold water for two days, changing the water twice a day. To every pound of cucumber allow one pound of sugar, two cupfuls of water, the thinly pared rind of one lemon and two or three pieces of slightly bruised whole ginger. Boil the sugar, water, ginger and lemon rind together for ten minutes, then put in the pieces of cucumber, allowing them to remain for two weeks.

Every two or three days pour off the syrup and re-boil it, each time adding a little more sugar, so that at the last a thick, strong syrup is obtained. Be careful always to have the syrup quite cold before pouring it again over the pieces of cucumber. At the end of the two weeks put the cucumbers and syrup into sterilized jars and cover.

PRESERVED CURRANTS WITHOUT COOKING

1 quart currants   1½ lbs. (3 cups) sugar

Stem the currants and crush each berry with a silver fork; then to two cupfuls of crushed currants add three cupfuls of sugar and stir with a wooden spoon until well mixed. Allow to stand for twenty-four hours, stirring frequently, then fill into sterilized glasses and cover.

The preserve will ferment if each berry is not crushed.

Another Method: Press fresh fruit through a fruit

press or a colander fine enough to take out all the skins and seeds. Add an equal quantity of sugar and stir for thirty minutes with a wooden spoon. Be sure that the sugar is well dissolved, as that is the secret of success. Then pour the mixture into sterilized glasses and set away in a cool, dry place until a thin, sugary crust is formed over the top.

Then cover and keep in a cool place.

PRESERVED GINGER

Green ginger or dried ginger   Sugar
  roots

Cover the ginger well with water. If it is green soak for thirty minutes, but if the roots are dried allow one hour. Boil the green ginger for thirty minutes and the dried roots for one hour.

Slice the ginger and strain the water.

To one cupful of the water allow three-fourths of a cupful of sugar and boil for thirty minutes or until a rich syrup is formed. Add the sliced ginger and boil until clear.

Seal in jars.

PRESERVED ORANGES

Oranges   Sugar

Wash and dry any number of oranges, grate the outside rinds very slightly, just enough to remove the dark outside skin and break the oil cells. Put the

Jellies, Jams and Preserves

whole oranges into a preserving pan filled with very salt water and let soak over night. The water soaks out the oil and the salt toughens the skins. Soak again in fresh water for three hours. Then cut in half and squeeze the juice into a basin.

Boil the orange halves for fifteen minutes in clear water, then drain. Now strain the juice over the oranges, add one-half cupful of sugar to each orange, and boil the halves in the juice until tender.

Seal in jars.

PRESERVED PINEAPPLES

Sugar-loaf pineapples   Sugar

Select ripe pineapples. To test the ripeness pull one of the little pines sharply. If it comes out easily, the fruit is in the right condition for preserving. It is best to put up pineapples in a moderately heavy syrup. A good proportion is three-fourths of a pound of sugar to a pound of fruit measured after it has been peeled and cut into little pieces or shredded with a silver fork. As fast as the fruit is prepared, put it into a large stone jar, layer by layer, with three-fourths of its weight in sugar.

When all the pineapples are finished put a cover on the jar and let it stand in a cool place until the next morning. By that time the juice will have dissolved the sugar and a clear syrup will cover the fruit.

Put the pineapple and the syrup into a preserving

kettle, bring slowly to boiling point, skim and simmer until tender, then can at once.

Time required in the cooking may vary from ten to thirty minutes, according to the ripeness of the fruit.

PRESERVED RASPBERRIES

Raspberries   Sugar
Water

Pick over the raspberries carefully and put them into clean jars. Allow cold water to run on to them, and rinse by turning the jar upside down and allowing the water to run out twice.

Lay the glass cover on the top of the jars, set on a dry tin, or on asbestos mats, in a moderate oven, and allow to heat through thoroughly. The oven must not be too hot, or the berries will cook too much and spoil in shape.

Have ready a syrup made by boiling two cupfuls of water with two cupfuls of sugar for twenty minutes, pour it into the jars, cover at once, and when cool brush around the rubber rings with melted paraffin.

PRESERVING FRUIT WITHOUT HEAT

Strawberries or peaches   Sugar

Prepare the fruit, and pack into sterilized jars as tightly as possible without crushing it. When the jars are about one-half full, fill up all the crevices

Jellies, Jams and Preserves

with sugar, then fill the jars to the tops with fruit and add all the sugar that can be shaken into them.

Cover with rubbers and tops and bury the jars in the ground.

The earth should be three inches above the tops of the jars.

Allow to remain in the ground for three months before using.

PRUNE AND ORANGE JAM

Prunes   Sugar
Oranges

Wash some prunes thoroughly in both hot and cold water, then cut from the pits. Put the meat through a food chopper and to each cupful of chopped prunes take one cupful of cut orange. Add the grated rinds of one-half of the oranges used. Add one tablespoonful of sugar to each cupful of orange, and to two cupfuls of prunes add one-half cupful of water.

Stir well together, stand in a saucepan at the back of the range, and let the jam simmer until thick.

Seal in jelly glasses.

PRUNE BUTTER

4 lbs. prunes   1 lemon
4 lbs. (8 cups) sugar

Wash the prunes thoroughly, soak them in cold water over night, then simmer until tender, remove the stones and rub through a sieve or press through a fruit press. Add the grated rind, the strained juice of the lemon and the sugar and cook until thick.

Seal in jars.

PRUNE MARMALADE

2½ lbs. prunes	1 lemon
6 large apples	1 orange
½ lb. (1 cup) sugar	

Select fine prunes, then wash and soak them in water over night. Steam or stew them gently until tender, using enough water to cover. Set aside until cool enough to handle; remove the pits.

Return to the pan, add the apples, pared, cored and sliced, the sugar, the strained juices of the orange and lemon, and cook to a marmalade, stirring occasionally that the mixture may be smooth.

Put into glasses or jars and cover at once.

PUMPKIN BUTTER

5 lbs. pumpkin	2 tablespoonfuls ground ginger
6 lbs. (12 cups) sugar	
6 lemons	2 tablespoonfuls ground cinnamon

Peel and cut fine the pumpkin, add the ginger, cinnamon and sugar and allow to stand over night.

Jellies, Jams and Preserves

Chop the lemons and cook till tender in a very little water, then add to other ingredients and boil until the pumpkin is transparent.

Seal in jars.

PUMPKIN MARMALADE

1 medium sized pumpkin	3 ozs. ginger root
2 lemons	1 teaspoonful tartaric acid
1 orange	Sugar

Peel and slice the pumpkin, then cut it into very small strips. Remove the seeds. Take two measures of pumpkin to one of sugar. Put the pumpkin and sugar into a preserving pan, add the orange and lemon rinds, cut into the smallest pieces, then bruise the ginger, put it into a muslin bag and add it. Let stand over night, then in the morning set on the stove and cook until thick. The tartaric acid is added about thirty minutes before the marmalade is ready.

Cover and seal.

QUINCE AND PUMPKIN PRESERVE

18 quinces	Sugar
Pumpkin	

Peel, quarter and remove the cores from the quinces. Weigh and put into a preserving pan, cover with water and cook slowly until tender. Take the same quantity of pumpkin, which has been peeled and cut into pieces about the same size as the quince quarters.

Scald well and drain. Now add to the quince its weight in sugar, the well-drained pumpkin, and the juice of the skins and the cores of the quinces, which have been well cooked in water and strained. Cook slowly until thick.

Seal in jars.

QUINCE BUTTER

Quinces   Sugar
Apples

Wash and rub the fuzz from the quinces, then peel and core, reserving the seeds and the parings. Cover them with water, simmer thirty minutes, then strain through a fine sieve or drip bag.

Put the small pieces of sliced quince in this, adding a little more water if necessary. Cook gently until nearly soft, then add about the same amount of good cooking apples, peeled and cored.

Their cores and parings can be cooked with those of the quinces.

When the quinces and apples are sufficiently soft, force them through a fruit press, adding a little water if too stiff to mash through easily. Cook this mixture, stirring frequently with a wooden spoon, until quite thick, then add half its bulk in granulated sugar, and cook slowly for one and one-half hours.

Turn into jars and seal.

Jellies, Jams and Preserves

QUINCE JELLY

Quinces	Water
Sugar	

In making quince jelly, cover the parings and the cores from the quinces with cold water, adding as many more whole quinces cut in small pieces, without paring, as are needed.

Simmer for several hours, adding more water as it cooks away. While the use of the seeds darkens the jelly somewhat, they contain so much of the pectose, or jellying principle, that most housekeepers prefer to use them. When reduced to a soft pulp, pour into a jelly bag and let drain over night. In the morning, boil the juice for twenty minutes, while the sugar, pound for pound, is heating in the oven.

At the end of twenty minutes, turn the sugar in with the juice, stir until dissolved, remove the spoon, cook for five minutes longer, then turn into glasses and seal when cold.

QUINCE PRESERVES

15 large ripe quinces	5 lbs. (10 cups) sugar
1 peck sweet apples	1 pint (2 cups) water

Wipe the quinces and the apples. Pare and quarter the apples, pare and core the quinces, cut them into eighths and place the fruit in a preserving pan in alternate layers with the sugar; add the water and allow to stand over night.

In the morning place the pan over the fire and cook until the fruit is tender and the syrup clear. Seal in jars.

RASPBERRY AND APPLE JAM

2 lbs. raspberries   3 lbs. lump sugar
4 lbs. apples   1 pint (2 cups) water

Peel and core the apples, cut them in thin slices, and put them into a preserving pan with the sugar and the water. Place on the fire, bring to boiling point and boil for fifteen minutes; then remove to the side of the range and let simmer. Pick the raspberries, add them and let the jam simmer until it jellies.

Seal in glasses.

RASPBERRY JAM

Ripe raspberries   Sugar
White currants

Pick off the stalks and set aside half the raspberries, choosing the best, the remainder, with one-half pound of white currants to each pound of berries, crush in a cloth so as to get out all the juice. Put the juice in a porcelain-lined pan with three-fourths of a pound of sugar to every pound of juice and allow the same quantity for every remaining pound of berries.

Boil the sugar and juice for twenty minutes, skimming carefully, then put in the whole fruit and boil for ten minutes longer, testing a little on a saucer.

For Rhubarb and Fig Marmalade

Jellies, Jams and Preserves

Divide into sterilized jars and cover with melted paraffin.

Another Method: Take two cupfuls of red currant juice and place it in a preserving pan with seven pounds of sugar. Bring to boiling point, stirring steadily all the time. As soon as the syrup boils add six pounds of picked ripe raspberries and continue to boil for twenty minutes.

RASPBERRY JELLY

Raspberries   Sugar

Pick and weigh the raspberries, place them in a large covered jar, stand the jar in a saucepan of boiling water, and cook gently for one hour, then strain through a fruit press or strainer.

Measure the juice and to each pint allow three-fourths of a pound of sugar. Boil for twenty minutes, then add the heated sugar and boil for five minutes longer.

Pour into glasses and seal.

RHUBARB AND FIG MARMALADE

4 lbs. rhubarb   2 ozs. almonds
2 lbs. dried figs   1 lemon
3 lbs. lump sugar

Wash and dry the rhubarb, cut into inch pieces and cook it for fifteen minutes with one-half cupful of water. Wash and dry the figs, blanch the almonds, and pass both through a food chopper.

Add the sugar and boil all together for thirty minutes. Add the strained lemon juice, pour into jars, and seal when cold.

Another Method: Wash and dry one pound of figs and three pounds of rhubarb, then cut them into small pieces and put them into a basin with three pounds of sugar, the grated rind and strained juice of one lemon. Mix and allow to stand over night. Put into a preserving pan and simmer for thirty minutes.

Seal while hot.

RHUBARB AND GINGER PRESERVE NO. 1

4 lbs. rhubarb	½ lb. preserved ginger
4 lbs. (8 cups) sugar	1 gill (½ cup) water
½ lb. candied lemon peel	

Choose firm, red stalks of rhubarb; wash and dry well with a cloth. Cut in six inch lengths and lay them on platters to dry for two days. Chop the lemon peel and ginger and put them into a preserving pan with sugar and water. Boil for five minutes, then add rhubarb and let boil for thirty minutes, stirring as little as possible.

Seal in glasses.

RHUBARB AND GINGER PRESERVE NO. 2

Rhubarb	Sugar
Ginger	

Rhubarb and ginger preserve is delicious. To every three pounds of rhubarb allow one-half pound of preserved ginger and two pounds of sugar. Wash and dry the rhubarb and cut it into pieces. Put these with the chopped ginger into an earthenware jar, add the sugar and set aside for two days.

Then pour off the liquid thus obtained into a preserving pan and boil gently for ten minutes. Add the rhubarb and ginger, and boil, not too quickly, for fifteen minutes.

The rhubarb should be weighed after it has been cut up.

Seal in jars.

RHUBARB AND PRUNE CONSERVE

4 lbs. rhubarb	3 lemons
2 lbs. prunes	4 lbs. sugar

Wash the prunes, then cover them with water and allow to soak for twenty-four hours. Wash, dry, and cut the rhubarb into small pieces, and sprinkle over it one pound of the sugar. Now place the prunes, the water in which they were soaked, and the rhubarb, into a preserving pan.

Wash the lemons, cut them in quarters, add, and simmer for one hour. Add the remainder of the sugar and boil for one-half hour longer.

Remove the lemons and seal the conserve in glasses.

8

RHUBARB AND STRAWBERRY PRESERVE

2 quarts rhubarb	1 lb. (2 cups) sugar
1 pint (2 cups) strawberries	1 pinch baking soda

Wash and dry the rhubarb, cut in small pieces, then stew it in a little water, and when almost done add the strawberries. Cook for three minutes, then add sugar and soda.

Seal in glasses.

If rhubarb jelly refuses to "jell" it is wise to add a little tartaric acid or the white rind of an orange.

RHUBARB BUTTER

1 gallon rhubarb	1 lemon
1 lb. raisins	2 lbs. (4 cups) sugar
3 oranges	

Chop the rhubarb, raisins, oranges and lemon, put into a preserving kettle with the sugar, and cook for one hour or until the butter is nearly smooth.

Pour into jars and seal.

(PIEPLANT) RHUBARB MARMALADE

4 lbs. rhubarb	¾ lb. blanched chopped al-
1 gill (½ cup) water	monds
5 lemons	1 oz. bottle ginger extract
6 lbs. (12 cups) sugar	

Wash and dry the rhubarb and cut in small pieces, add water, chopped rinds of lemons, and boil twenty minutes. Now add the sugar, almonds, and ginger extract, and boil rapidly until clear.

It takes from fifteen to twenty minutes. Put into jars and seal.

Another Method: Cut two pounds of rhubarb into small pieces, add one and one-half pounds sugar, rinds and pulp of six oranges and one lemon and put into a preserving pan. Boil down until the mass is thick and smooth, stirring frequently.

RIPE TOMATO CONSERVE

Ripe tomatoes   Lemons
Sugar

Peel the tomatoes, press them and throw away as much as possible of the seeds and juice.

To seven pounds of the firm fruit add five pounds of sugar, and cook slowly together for about two hours. Just before it is done, add four washed lemons cut up fine. Reject the seeds.

Skim out the tomatoes and boil down the syrup.

When thick pour it over the fruit and seal in sterilized jars.

ROSE HIP JELLY

Rose hips   Sugar

Gather the hips when they are red and plump, then wash and dry them. Cut them in halves lengthwise with a sharp penknife, and remove the pips and little hairs.

Weigh the skins and put them into a preserving pan with just enough water to keep them from burning. Cover and cook until tender, then strain without pressure

Measure the liquid and boil it for ten minutes, then add two cupfuls of sugar to each pint of juice and boil until the syrup jellies on a spoon.

If preferred, the sugar, water and fruit may be cooked together until the hips are soft. It is then strained.

Another Method: Stew the prepared hips in a little water until tender. Weigh them and take the same weight of vegetable marrow, cut in small pieces; add nearly the combined weight of both in lump sugar, and boil for thirty minutes.

Seal in small glasses.

ROSE LEAF CONSERVE

Rose leaves	Water or rose water
Sugar	Orange flower water

Cut the roses when in full bloom, pull out the petals, and spread on a tray to dry. Make a syrup with two pounds of lump sugar and as little water or rose water as possible

Weigh two pounds of dried rose leaves, wash them for a minute in boiling water; then drain and dry,

Jellies, Jams and Preserves

and add them to the syrup with two tablespoonfuls of orange flower water; cook until thick, then pour into small jars and seal.

Or the rose leaves may be put into a porcelain-lined pan with just enough water to cover them, covered and cooked slowly until tender, when the sugar may be added and all boiled gently until a syrup is formed.

These leaves make attractive decorations for icings and candies, and they are also a delightful addition to cake batter, puddings, sauces and mince meat.

SACCHARINE MARMALADE

3 lbs. bitter oranges	Saccharine
3 quarts water	½ tablespoonful powdered
2 lemons	gelatine
6 lbs. (12 cups) sugar	

Pare the oranges as thinly as possible, cut the peel into small shreds, and tie these shreds up loosely in a muslin bag.

Quarter the peeled oranges, and squeeze out the juice, reserving this. Now boil the pulp and the shreds very slowly in the water until the liquid is reduced to three pints. Strain and put back into the preserving pan with the juice, grated rinds and strained juice of the lemons, the shreds of the oranges, the gelatine and the sugar, or its equivalent in saccharine, simmer very slowly for thirty minutes, by which time it should be fairly sweet and transparent.

It must be remembered when using saccharine as a substitute for sugar that it is three hundred times as sweet as the latter, so that it is absolutely essential to measure it carefully and dissolve it thoroughly; twenty-six grains of saccharine are equivalent to one pound of sugar, and it is usually sold in tabloids weighing as nearly as possible two grains, so that thirteen of these tabloids go to one pound of sugar. When sold in powder it is usually accompanied by a small measure, which when filled level represents two grains. If not thoroughly dissolved there will be tiny atoms of the most nauseating sweetness through the marmalade. The gelatine is added to give body and stiffness to the preserve. Saccharine with the addition of the gelatine can be substituted for sugar in many cases.

SCOTCH MARMALADE

| 12 firm oranges | Sugar |
| 6 ripe lemons | |

Wash and dry the oranges and lemons, then slice them as thin as possible, removing the seeds. Put them into a preserving pan with three pints of cold water to every pound of fruit. Let stand for twenty-four hours, then boil until tender and let stand for another twenty-four hours.

Jellies, Jams and Preserves

Add one and one-fourth pounds of sugar to every pound of boiled fruit, and boil until the chips are transparent and the syrup will jelly.

Remove from the fire and when cold put into glasses and cover with paraffin.

Another Method: Nine bitter oranges, four lemons, three sweet oranges, four quarts of water, eight pounds of crushed lump sugar, and one wineglassful of brandy. Cut across the grain of the oranges and the lemons as finely as possible, place in a deep crock, add the water, and allow to stand for forty-eight hours, then add the sugar and boil for one hour, adding the brandy when nearly done.

SPICED CRANBERRIES

5 lbs. cranberries	1 tablespoonful ground all-
3½ lbs. (7 cups) brown sugar	spice
1 pint (2 cups) vinegar	1 tablespoonful ground
1 tablespoonful ground cinnamon	cloves
	½ tablespoonful ground ginger

Boil the sugar, vinegar and spices for twenty minutes, then add the cranberries and boil slowly for two hours.

Seal in jars.

SPICED CURRANTS

5 lbs. stemmed currants
4 lbs. (8 cups) sugar
1 pint (2 cups) vinegar
1 tablespoonful powdered
   cinnamon

1 tablespoonful powdered
   ginger
1 tablespoonful powdered
   allspice
1 tablespoonful powdered
   cloves

Put the currants, sugar, vinegar and spices into a preserving kettle, allow to boil, then simmer gently for forty minutes.

Pour into glasses and seal.

SPICED FIGS

Figs
½ pint (1 cup) vinegar
4 sticks cinnamon
1 tablespoonful cloves

1 teaspoonful allspice
1¼ lbs. (2½ cups) brown
   sugar
1 teaspoonful mace

For the spiced figs, buy the loose figs rather than those which have been pressed, though the latter may be used. If the dried figs are used soak them over night in water, then drain.

Boil the vinegar and sugar until thick, add the cinnamon broken in small pieces, cloves, allspice, and mace, then add the figs, allow to simmer slowly for one and one-fourth hours, pour into jars, and seal.

Spiced Fruits: To eight pounds of fruit allow four

Jellies, Jams and Preserves

pounds of sugar, one pint of good vinegar, one table-spoonful of ground cinnamon, one tablespoonful of ground allspice, one tablespoonful of ground ginger, one teaspoonful of ground mace, one teaspoonful of ground cloves, one tablespoonful of grated nutmeg and six crushed bay leaves; mix the spices, put them in four muslin bags and tie them loosely. Boil the sugar and the vinegar for five minutes, add the spices and the fruit and cook until the fruit is tender. Soft fruit must not remain long on the fire. Remove from the fire and cool.

Next morning lift the fruit with a skimmer and put it into glass or stone jars. Boil the syrup, pour it over the fruit and let cool; do this for nine mornings. This recipe will answer for pears, peaches, apples, currants, apricots, watermelon rind, citron melon and cantaloupes.

SPICED GRAPES

Grapes	Cloves
Brown sugar	Mace
Powdered cinnamon	Vinegar

Remove the skins from the grapes. To five quarts of skins add three pounds of brown sugar, two table-spoonfuls of powdered cinnamon, one tablespoonful powdered cloves, one tablespoonful powdered mace and one cupful of vinegar, and cook slowly one and one-half hours; then mash through a sieve or press through fruit press. Remove any seeds from the pulps, add one-half cupful of vinegar, put into a preserving kettle, cook until soft, and add to rest of mixture.

Seal in jars.

SPICED PEACHES

7 lbs. peaches	½ oz. cloves
1 pint (2 cups) vinegar	2 ozs. broken cinnamon
3 lbs. (6 cups) sugar	½ oz. allspice

Scald the vinegar, sugar and spices, then pour over the peaches. Allow to stand for twenty-four hours, drain off, scald again, and pour over the fruit, then let stand again for twenty-four hours.

Boil all together until the peaches are tender, then put the peaches into jars.

Boil the syrup until thickened, then pour over the fruit and seal.

SPICED QUINCES

7 lbs. quinces	2 teaspoonfuls ground all-spice
4 lbs. (8 cups) sugar	
1 pint (2 cups) vinegar	2 teaspoonfuls ground cinnamon
½ oz. ginger root	
1 teaspoonful ground cloves	½ teaspoonful ground mace

Pare and core the quinces. Put the vinegar and sugar on to boil. Mix spices and divide into four parts. Put each into a little square of muslin, tie tightly, then throw them in with sugar and vinegar. When mixture is hot add quinces; bring all to boiling point, remove from fire and turn carefully into stone jar.

Stand in cool place over night.

Next morning drain all the liquor from the quinces into preserving kettle; stand it over moderate fire, and when boiling hot pour it back in jar over quinces.

Next day drain and heat again as before; do this for nine consecutive days; the last time boil the liquor down until there is just sufficient to cover fruit.

Add the fruit to it; bring the whole to a boil, divide into jars and seal

SPICED RHUBARB

Rhubarb	1 teaspoonful ground cinnamon
Onions	
1 pint (2 cups) vinegar	1 teaspoonful ground cloves
1 pint (2 cups) brown sugar	1 teaspoonful ground allspice
1 teaspoonful salt	
1 teaspoonful ground ginger	½ teaspoonful grated nutmeg

Wash some rhubarb, peel it if necessary, and cut it in pieces.

Measure five quarts and stew till soft in a little water, then add one cupful of chopped onions, vinegar, sugar, salt and spices.

Boil all together till fairly thick, stirring occasionally to prevent burning.

Put into jars and seal.

STRAWBERRY BAR-LE-DUC

Perfect strawberries   Sugar

Three things are indispensable in making strawberry bar-le-duc. The first is strong, steady sunshine, the second, hot platters or plates, the third plenty of window-glass.

The fruit should be of good flavor, the sugar pure. To every pound of fruit allow three cupfuls of sugar. Heat the sugar on plates in the oven, taking care not to let it melt or get too brown. It should be as hot as possible without melting.

Spread a thin layer of hot sugar over the bottoms of hot platters or deep plates, then a layer of fruit and then another layer of sugar.

Cover the platters with a clean sheet of window-glass and place outdoors in the hot sun or in a sunny window. If the fruit is outdoors it must be brought in when the sun sets and put in a dry place indoors.

Return to the sun in the morning. In a few days the fruit will grow plump and firm and the syrup almost a jelly.

Pack in tumblers and seal.

If the syrup is not thick, boil until clear and thickened, then pour in the glasses over the fruit.

Jellies, Jams and Preserves

STRAWBERRY CONSERVE

1 quart ripe strawberries	2 oranges
½ lb. seeded raisins	½ lb. chopped walnut meats
1 lemon	1 quart sugar

Wash and drain the strawberries, then put them into a preserving kettle with the raisins, sugar, grated rinds and pulp of the lemon and oranges. Cook slowly for thirty minutes, then add the walnuts and cook for ten minutes longer.

Put into tumblers and cover with melted paraffin.

Peaches, plums, grapes and cranberries may be used in place of strawberries.

STRAWBERRY JAM

Strawberries	Red currant juice
Lump sugar	Water

Take equal weights of strawberries and broken lump sugar, and to every four pounds of strawberries add two cupfuls of red currant juice and one cupful of water. When currant juice cannot be procured, dissolved red currant jelly may be used. Sieve the sugar until one-half its weight is free from lumps.

Place the strawberries, which should be dry and not overripe, on a dish, in layers, with the powdered part of the sugar, and allow to stand for twenty-four hours. On the following morning put the remainder of the sugar, red currant juice and the water into a preserving pan, stir until the sugar is dissolved, bring gently to boiling point and then simmer for thirty minutes, or until the syrup runs from the spoon in a thread.

Put in the fruit, bring slowly to boiling point, turning the fruit over gently from time to time, and boil until the syrup quickly stiffens on a cold saucer.

Pour into jelly glasses and seal.

STRAWBERRY JELLY

Underripe strawberries   Sugar

Use firm, perfect, slightly underripe fruit. Put into a preserving pan and let stand on the back of the range until the juice may be pressed out. Strain, and to each pint of juice allow one pound of sugar. Boil the juice for twenty minutes, add the sugar, which should have been heated in the oven, and boil for fifteen minutes longer.

Seal when cold.

STRAWBERRY PRESERVES

Dark red firm strawberries   Sugar

Hull the berries, place them on a sieve, sprinkle with water to remove the grit, and then allow to drain. Measure two and one-half cupfuls of berries. Put two cupfuls of sugar and one-half cupful of water into a saucepan and bring to boiling point, then add the berries and allow them to heat through. Boil

Jellies, Jams and Preserves

quickly for ten minutes, shaking the pan from side to side but do not stir with a spoon.

Remove from the fire, and, with a sterilized spoon or fork, lift the berries into glasses, filling them three-fourths full. Boil the syrup for five minutes longer, then pour over the berries, filling up the glasses nearly full.

Allow to stand for some time, or until the berries have settled; [then fill up with any of the left-over syrup.

Cover with melted paraffin and glass covers.

SWEET POTATO BUTTER

10 lbs. mashed sweet pota-toes	2½ pints (5 cups) water
	Seasonings to taste
5 lbs. (10 cups) sugar	

Boil the sweet potatoes until ready, then skin and mash them. Bring the sugar and water to boiling point and boil for fifteen minutes, add the mashed potatoes and simmer for three hours.

Flavor or season to taste.

Divide into jars, cover, and seal.

SUN PRESERVED CHERRIES

Tart cherries   Sugar

Pit and weigh some moderately tart cherries, and for each pound take seven-eighths pound of sugar. Put the cherries and sugar in layers in a large preserving kettle and allow to stand for ten minutes. Cook only three quarts of the fruit at a time.

Bring quickly to boil, then boil for five minutes. Pour into large platters and place out-of-doors in a hot sun for nine hours.

Divide into glass jars and cover with melted paraffin.

SUN PRESERVED STRAWBERRIES

2 lbs. ripe strawberries   ½ pint (1 cup) water
1 lb. (2 cups) sugar

Wash and pick the berries carefully. Boil the sugar and water together for eight minutes; drop in the strawberries and boil for two minutes. Remove from the fire, and spread the berries one layer thick in large platters.

Cover with netting and place out in the sun for three or four days until the syrup is thick. Bring in doors at night.

Put into sterilized jars, cover with melted paraffin, and seal.

Strawberries preserved in this manner retain their original shape, color and flavor.

Another Method: Put six cupfuls of granulated sugar and one pint of boiling water into a preserving kettle. Stir until the sugar is dissolved, heat to boiling point, let boil rapidly, without stirring, until the syrup will spin a thread when dropped from a fork. Pick, wash, drain, and hull sound, ripe straw-berries; weigh three pounds. Heat to the boiling point, and let simmer for twenty minutes. Pour out on large clean platters, cover with glass, and let stand in the sun for three days, turning the fruit over three times each day. The platters should be moved from time to time, that the direct rays of the sun may fall upon the fruit. Fill glasses to overflowing and seal.

TANGERINE MARMALADE

24 tangerines   Sugar
2 lemons

Wash and dry the tangerines and lemons, then put them into an enameled pan with sufficient water to float them, and let them boil until the rinds are soft enough to pierce with a needle; then drain them.

Quarter the oranges, remove the pips, let them soak in two cupfuls of water for twelve hours, and cut up the peel very fine, having removed all the pulp and mashed it up.

Put the sugar into a preserving pan, allowing double the weight of the fruit in sugar, add the water from the pips and the strained lemon juice, and boil to a thick syrup; then add the pulp and rinds, and boil till the syrup jellies, which will take from twenty-five to thirty-five minutes.

Seal in glasses.

9

TOMATO GINGER PRESERVES

Slightly underripe tomatoes   Ginger root
Alum   Sugar

Select large round tomatoes. Wash them in cold water and then cut in halves at right angles to the stems. Remove the seeds and throw tomato halves into alum water, allowing one ounce of alum to one-half gallon of water.

Weigh the tomatoes, allow as many pints of water as there are pounds, and one ounce of bruised ginger root to each pint of water; boil the ginger and water together until quite strong, then add one pound of granulated sugar for each pound of tomatoes and boil to a syrup.

Now add the tomatoes and cook gently for two hours, or until the fruit is rather dark. Remove the tomatoes and turn them into jars, boiling down the syrup until it is quite thick before pouring it over them; place a small piece of the ginger on the top of each jar and seal at once.

TOMATO JELLY

Ripe tomatoes   Sugar

Choose ripe, sound tomatoes, quarter them, and place them in a preserving pan over a bright fire until the juice runs freely; then strain and measure and for each pint of juice allow one pound of sugar.

Jellies, Jams and Preserves

Put the juice into a clean preserving pan and boil for thirty minutes, then add the sugar, which should be heated, and boil for ten minutes.

Pour into glasses and seal.

TOMATO MARMALADE

1 quart ripe tomatoes	1 lemon
2 lbs. (4 cups) sugar	2 oranges

Cut the peel of the lemon and oranges into small strips, then boil in a little water until tender and drain. Put the lemon and orange pulp into a preserving pan, add the sugar and the tomatoes peeled and cut into small pieces. Now add the peels and cook for two hours, stirring frequently.

The marmalade should be quite thick and the peel transparent.

Seal in small jars.

Yellow tomatoes make a beautiful marmalade.

Another Method: Tomato marmalade has the charm of novelty to commend it. Peel, quarter and remove the seeds from seven pounds of tomatoes. Slice rather small, and put into a basin with four cupfuls of water to stand all night.

Boil the seeds and skins with three cupfuls of water and the rinds and strained juice of two lemons, or if lemon flavoring is not liked, cloves, ginger or cinnamon might be substituted.

Strain through a jelly bag. Next day put this

juice, with the water off the tomatoes, in a preserving pan, and allow to boil fast for ten minutes. Add the tomatoes, boil till tender, but not pulpy, then add seven pounds of lump sugar, and allow all to boil till it will set—about fifteen minutes.

Divide into sterilized jars and seal.

TO PRESERVE FRUITS WITH HONEY

Fruit	Water
Sugar	Honey

Make a rich syrup, allowing one-half cupful of sugar and one-fourth pound of honey to each one and one-half pints of water. This is just sufficient for one quart jar.

Boil the syrup down one-third and skim carefully. While the syrup is boiling, rinse the jar inside and outside with hot water, pack the whole fruit in the jars, fasten the lids part way, set in a rack, then put at the back of the range where they will keep hot.

When the syrup is ready pour it over the fruit and seal.

VEGETABLE MARROW JAM

3 lbs. vegetable marrow	1 oz. ground ginger
3 lbs. lump sugar	2 lemons

Peel the vegetable marrow and remove the pips. Cut into pieces about two inches long and weigh. Put into a preserving pan, add the strained lemon juice and lemon rinds cut very thin, the sugar and the ginger.

Boil until clear, which should take about an hour.

Seal in glasses.

Another Method: Take six pounds of vegetable marrow, three chilies, two ounces of ginger root, two lemons and three-fourths of a pound of sugar to each pound of marrow. After peeling and removing the seeds of the marrow, cut it into small pieces.

Put the marrow and sugar into a preserving pan, and allow it to stand for twelve hours before boiling, then add the ginger (well bruised), the chilies tied in a muslin bag, the lemon rinds and the strained juice of the lemons. Boil the jam from three to four hours, and when done, remove the muslin bag and the lemon rinds.

Seal in jars.

VEGETABLE MARROW MARMALADE

Vegetable marrows	Lemons
Green ginger	Red pepper
Sugar	Brown sugar

To each pound of pared and seeded marrow allow one ounce of green ginger, grated or chopped fine, one pound of granulated sugar, the pared yellow rinds of two lemons cut into shreds and a few grains of red pepper.

Make a syrup with one pound of brown sugar and one cupful of water.

Chop the pared marrow and cover it with the brown sugar syrup. Let stand for two days, then drain off the syrup, which may be used again for the same purpose.

Make a heavy syrup with the granulated sugar, lemon rind, strained lemon juice, red pepper and ginger, allowing one-fourth of a cupful of water for each pound of sugar. Add the marrow and simmer slowly and steadily until it is clear and cooked to a marmalade.

Seal in small glasses.

WILD GRAPE AND ELDERBERRY JELLY

Wild grapes   Sugar
Elderberries

Add four pints of green grape juice and pulp to eight pints of elderberry juice. Strain them and add one pound of sugar to each pint of juice. Boil for twenty minutes or until the liquid jellies.

Pour into sterilized jelly glasses and cover when cold.

WILD GRAPE BUTTER

Wild grapes   Sugar
Apples

Pick the wild grapes after the frost has ripened them. Stem, mash, and mix them with an equal quantity of stewed and mashed apples. Press the mixture

Jellies, Jams and Preserves

through a fruit press, add half as much sugar as there is pulp and cook until thick, being careful that it does not burn.

Turn into stone jars and cover.

Another Method: Boil skins of five pounds of grapes until tender. Cook pulps until soft, then strain; add the skins, three pounds of sugar, two teaspoonfuls of powdered cloves, two teaspoonfuls of powdered allspice, one-half teaspoonful of powdered cinnamon, one-half teaspoonful of powdered ginger and one pint of vinegar and boil until thick.

WILD GRAPE JELLY

Wild grapes   Sugar

Pick the grapes as soon as they begin to change color. Crush the fruit and cook until very tender and broken. Turn into a jelly bag and let it drain over night.

In the morning boil the juice for thirty minutes, skimming frequently. Allow six cupfuls of sugar to two quarts of the juice, add it and boil until liquid jellies.

Divide into glasses and seal.

WINEBERRY JELLY

Wineberries   Sugar

Pick the berries and put them without water in the inner section of a double boiler. In the outer section put cold water and set on the fire until the berries are heated and soft. Mash and strain and boil the juice for twenty minutes, then add an equal quantity of heated sugar, stir until dissolved, and bring quickly to a boil.

Pour at once into hot jelly glasses and seal.

YELLOW TOMATO PRESERVE

Yellow tomatoes	Crystallized citron peel
Sugar	Lemons
Preserved ginger	

Tomato preserves made from the yellow tomato are excellent.

Use two cupfuls of sugar for each pound of tomatoes. Wash the tomatoes, plunge them in boiling water, allow them to remain for an instant then drain and remove the skins.

Place the tomatoes in an earthenware jar, add the sugar, cover the jar and allow the contents to stand over night.

In the morning drain off the syrup and boil it for five minutes, skimming it frequently. Add the tomatoes; and for each pound of tomatoes add two ounces of chopped preserved ginger, two ounces of chopped crystallized citron peel and two thinly sliced seeded lemons.

Simmer until the tomatoes are thoroughly cooked.

Seal in sterilized jars.

Jellies, Jams and Preserves

Another Method: Yellow tomatoes with an equal quantity of grated pineapple make an excellent preserve. Scald, peel and weigh the tomatoes, and to each pound use two cupfuls of sugar. Put the tomatoes, sugar and pineapple into a porcelain-lined pan and simmer for three hours.

Divide into sterilized tumblers or jars and cover with melted paraffin.

BRANDIED APRICOTS

Apricots   Brandy
Sugar

Wipe off the down from the fruit, and prick each apricot to the stone with a needle. Put them into a saucepan, and scald with boiling water. Cover for five minutes, then take them out to drain and dry.

To one dozen large apricots allow two cupfuls of sugar. Make a clear syrup, composed of one gill of water to every pound of sugar, and one white of egg. Put in the apricots, and let the fruit and syrup come to a boil. Remove from the fire, and allow the fruit to remain in the syrup until next day. In the morning take out the apricots and set the pan over the fire. When it has boiled for five minutes put in the apricots, and let the whole boil for five minutes longer. Then take out the fruit and allow it to become cold. Boil down the syrup to one-half its original quantity, taking care that it does not boil long enough to congeal or to become thick. Put the apricots into a glass jar, and pour the syrup over them.

Fill up the jar with the best brandy, and seal at once.

BRANDIED CHERRIES

Cherries	Coriander seeds
Brandy	Anise seeds
Cloves	A rich sugar syrup

Select large ripe cherries, let the stems remain on, make a small hole with a large needle at the ends opposite to the stems, put them into cold water, then drain and place in clean jars.

Pour over them a rich syrup of boiling sugar and allow to remain for one day in this, then drain this off entirely and boil it again, adding two cupfuls of the syrup to two pints of the best brandy.

Pour this over the fruit, and on the top of each jar place a muslin bag containing one-fourth of an ounce of cloves, one-half ounce of coriander seeds and one-half ounce of anise seeds.

Cork up tightly and expose to the sun for four weeks, then remove the spice bags, cork again and shake the jars so that all of the aromatic flavor will be imparted to the syrup.

When taking out the cherries for use be careful to cork the mouth of the jar in order to exclude the air.

Jellies, Jams and Preserves

BRANDIED GREEN GAGES

12 lbs. green gages	1 pint (2 cups) water
8 lbs. (16 cups) sugar	6 pints (12 cups) brandy

Choose large, fine specimens of the fruit. Rinse them in cold water, then drain and with a needle stick each one around the stem.

Boil the sugar and water together till a clear syrup is formed, removing the scum. Drop in the gages and boil for two minutes.

Remove the saucepan from the fire, pour its contents into a large earthenware bowl, cover tightly, and let stand for forty-eight hours. Remove the gages from the syrup, return it to the kettle, place over the fire, and allow to boil until it will form a soft ball when tested in cold water, or 240° by the thermometer.

Remove from the fire and add the brandy. Pack the gages evenly in sterilized glass jars. Fill them to overflowing with the syrup, then cover at once.

The green gages will be ready in six weeks.

BRANDIED PEACHES

Peaches	Brandy
Sugar	

Make a syrup of eight cupfuls of sugar and two pints of water. Let it come to boiling point, then cook for eight minutes, and add four pounds of peeled peaches. Cook for five minutes longer, then skim out the peaches and pack them in sterilized glass jars. Boil the syrup until it thickens, add two cupfuls of brandy, and pour at once into the jars.

Cover and seal.

Pears may be brandied in the same way.

AMBROSIA OR TUTTI FRUTTI

1 pint (2 cups) brandy   Sugar
Various ripe fruits

Put the brandy into a large stone jar, and add the various fruits as they come in season. To each quart of fruit add the same quantity of sugar; then stir the mixture with a wooden spoon each day until all the fruits have been added.

Raspberries, oranges, currants, cherries, strawberries, bananas, pears, plums, apricots, peaches, pineapples and apples are the best fruits to use.

Apricots, peaches, pineapples, apples, bananas, pears and plums should be cut in small pieces.

Keep covered with a cloth and a tight fitting cover.

This ambrosia is delicious to serve with ice creams, frozen puddings, sauces, cornstarch puddings and jellies.

CANDIED CHERRIES

Cherries   Pinch cream of tartar
Sugar   Water

Stone ripe cherries, saving any juice.

Put into a saucepan one pint of water and two

Jellies, Jams and Preserves

cupfuls of sugar, and stir until the sugar is dissolved, then add cream of tartar and boil until it forms a thick syrup, skim, add the cherries and cook slowly until tender. Drain well, then place on platters to dry, or in baking tins lined with white paper and dry in a slow oven, changing the paper quite often.

When free from moisture, pack in boxes which have been lined with waxed paper, placing waxed paper between each layer of fruit, and sprinkling well with sugar. Put on the cover of the box, then wrap the box securely in paper and put away in a dry place.

These are delicious served by themselves, or used in candies, puddings, cakes and sauces.

CANDIED GRAPE-FRUIT PEEL

Grape-fruit peel	1¾ lbs. (3½ cups) sugar
1½ cups (¾ lb.) salt	¾ pint (1½ cups) water

Wash and dry a few grape-fruit peels, then cut them with scissors or a sharp knife into strips. Measure two quarts of the rinds, mix with the salt and allow to stand for twenty-four hours. Drain and rinse in cold water, then cover with fresh water, simmer for four hours, and drain once more.

Put the sugar and water into a large saucepan and boil to a thick syrup or to 230° F.; now add the peels and simmer until the syrup is almost absorbed. Be careful not to burn.

Set aside to cool slightly, then remove the rinds with a silver fork on to a platter of granulated sugar and roll them about in it.

Drop them on to waxed paper to dry.

CANDIED ORANGE PEEL

1 lb. orange peel	2 lbs. (4 cups) sugar
3 pints (6 cups) water	½ teaspoonful powdered ginger

Soak the peels in salted water, changing each night for five nights. Slice into strips and boil in the sugar, water and powdered ginger until the syrup is thick. Remove from the fire, beat well, and spread the candied peel on buttered sheets of paper. Allow the sugared syrup to form a hard crust on each piece.

These should be curled up and crisp when thoroughly dry.

Pack in boxes between waxed paper.

CANDIED PEARS

Pears	Water
Sugar	

Peel, core and halve the pears. Have ready and boiling a thick syrup made with one cupful of water to each two cupfuls of sugar. Drop the pears in this and let them cook until tender, but not broken. Remove from the fire and let them stand as they are for two days. Then remove and drain the pears, and sprinkle sugar over each piece separately.

Jellies, Jams and Preserves

Dry them slowly in the sun or in a very moderate oven with the door partly open.

Pack in jars and cover.

CANDIED PLUMS

2 lbs. plums   1 pint (2 cups) water
1 lb. (2 cups) sugar

Drop the plums, which must be large and perfect, in boiling water and cook for ten minutes, then drain thoroughly.

Make a syrup with the sugar and water and when it forms a soft ball put in the plums. Remove from the fire and let it stand over night in a slow oven, turning the fruit occasionally. Repeat this operation four times, each time skimming out the fruit and letting the syrup just come to a boil. The fifth time make a new syrup, as in the first place, and when it boils and stands the test put the fruit in again.

As soon as the syrup is cool, dip out the fruit and place in a pan to harden and candy, keeping it at a temperature of 65 degrees.

When sufficiently candied place in boxes between layers of waxed paper.

CANDIED PINEAPPLE

Pineapples   Sugar

Peel and cut pineapples in rather thick slices, remove the cores and cut the slices in halves, giving them a crescent shape. Allow one cupful of water to each pound of pineapple and cook slowly until tender and clear. Remove the fruit and add to the water a pound of sugar for each pound of fruit. Boil the syrup down one-third, then put in the fruit and cook until it is transparent.

Again carefully remove the slices, spread on platters and set in the sun. Cook the syrup down to a candy stage and pour over the fruit slices.

Let dry and pack away in wide glass jars with dry sugar or brandied papers between each layer.

Seal.

PUMPKIN CHIPS

Good high colored sweet pumpkins	Lemons
Sugar	Ginger

Peel and halve the pumpkins, take out the seeds and cut into thick chips. For each pound of pumpkin allow two cupfuls of sugar and one-half cupful of lemon juice.

Put the chips into a deep earthenware dish and sprinkle over each layer a layer of sugar. Pour the lemon juice over the whole.

Let it remain for a day, then boil together, allowing one cupful of water to each three pounds of pumpkin, one tablespoonful of bruised ginger tied in muslin bags, and the shredded peels of the lemons.

Jellies, Jams and Preserves

When the pumpkin becomes tender turn the whole into a stone jar and set away in a cool place for one week.

At the end of that time pour the syrup off the chips, boil down until rich and thick, then pour over the pumpkin and seal.

This makes a delicious sweetmeat.

QUINCE CHIPS

Quinces   Sugar

Pare, quarter and core ripe quinces, cut each quarter into thin slices, weigh, and to each pound allow one pound of sugar. Put the quince chips into a preserving pan, cover with boiling water, and boil quickly for ten minutes, then drain.

Put the chips back into the pan with the sugar; add one cupful of water, cover and stand on the back part of the range where the sugar will melt slowly and cook the quinces until they are dark red and transparent.

Lift each piece with a skimmer and place on waxed paper, on a sieve, to dry.

When dry, roll in granulated sugar and pack away in boxes with waxed paper between each layer.

STRIPED JELLY

Striped jelly is very popular at parties where refreshments a little out of the ordinary are desired.

10

Place a dark jelly, such as strawberry, in the bottom of a glass jar to the depth of one-half inch. Allow this to cool; it may even stand for a few weeks if necessary. Then pour on top of it a red jelly, such as currant jelly, and continue this process with as many shades as desired until the jar is full. Seal.

TO BOTTLE FRUIT WITHOUT SUGAR

Ripe damsons or plums	Tapers
Sealing wax or paraffin	New soft corks or lids

Take as many quarts of fruit as are required. The fruit should be ripe, but not overripe. It must be carefully selected, and handled as little as possible. Remove the stalks, and reject any fruit that has the skin broken.

The bottles must be spotlessly clean and absolutely dry.

When all is in readiness, light a taper and let it burn in the bottle for a few seconds—to exhaust the air; then pack the fruit quickly in. Cork or cover the bottle, and proceed with the others.

When all are filled, stand them in a very cool oven for several hours, until the fruit has shrunk away one-fourth part. Take the bottles out of the oven, press the corks well in, or adjust the lids.

If corks are used run hot sealing wax or melted paraffin over them. Store the bottles in a cool place.

Printed in Great Britain
by Amazon

72865314R00073